CONGRESS AT PRINCETON

Charles Thomson by Matthew Pratt
Oil on canvas. Collection of Armistead Peter, 3rd
Courtesy of the Frick Art Reference Library

Congress at Princeton

Being the Letters of Charles Thomson
to Hannah Thomson
June-October
1783

EDITED BY EUGENE R. SHERIDAN
AND JOHN M. MURRIN

PRINCETON UNIVERSITY LIBRARY
PRINCETON, NEW JERSEY
1985

Published under the sponsorship of
the Friends of the Princeton University Library

Printed in the United States of America
by Princeton University Press
at Princeton, New Jersey

ILLUSTRATIONS

❖

FOREWORD

❖

At Sotheby Parke Bernet, on 3 October 1978, these thirty-three letters by Charles Thomson to his wife Hannah were sold at public auction to a New York rare book dealer. In March 1983, Miss Jean F. Preston, Curator of Manuscripts in the Princeton University Library, brought them from New York to Princeton on approval. It took only a few hours of reading to convince ourselves that they had to stay here, particularly since the town and the university were soon to celebrate the 200th anniversary of the meeting of the Continental Congress in Nassau Hall, June-October 1783, four remarkable months during which Princeton served as the nation's capital. Charles Thomson had been Secretary of the Congress since its inception, and when it fled Philadelphia in June of 1783 he was among the first to leave for the little college town in New Jersey.

How to raise the purchase price was our next problem. Fortunately the Council of the Friends of the Library came to our aid by voting to ask the whole membership for the funds. Letters went out in early May. The response was so immediate and generous that within four weeks we had received, from all over the country, a sum large enough to insure purchase as well as eventual book publication. Meanwhile Nathaniel Burt, a member of the Council and a social historian, volunteered to write a sketch of Thomson and excerpt some of his more personal comments to his wife about life in New Jersey during a long hot summer. "Exile in Princeton: The Letters of Charles Thomson, 1783" appeared in the Autumn 1983 issue of the *Princeton University Library Chronicle*. It was offered as "an appetizer, presenting selections from many of the letters but no complete ones" and omitting "the more dense descriptions of political intrigue." Mr. Burt's prose not only whetted the appetite but led to the next logical step: finding the right editors for the full publication. They were on our doorstep.

Mr. Eugene R. Sheridan is associate editor of the *Papers of Thomas Jefferson*, having arrived here in 1981 from the Library of Congress. His *Lewis Morris, 1671-1746: A Study in Early American Politics* was published in 1981. Professor John M. Murrin has been teaching

Colonial American history at Princeton University since 1973. He is the editor, with Stanley N. Katz, of *Colonial America: Essays in Politics and Social Development*, third edition, 1983. After reading Thomson's prose they agreed with alacrity that they should share the editorial work on this book. Mr. Sheridan transcribed the text and prepared the much-needed footnotes; Professor Murrin joined him in writing the introduction.

For their congenial assumption of these tasks the staff of the Department of Rare Books and Special Collections is deeply grateful. To the unfailing generosity of the Friends of the Library we all, once again, are indebted.

Richard M. Ludwig

Assistant University Librarian for
Rare Books and Special Collections

INTRODUCTION

❖

Charles Thomson is hardly remembered today except by those who specialize in the study of the American Revolution and the history of biblical translation. But he was once one of the best known Patriot leaders during the epochal conflict with Great Britain that gave birth to the new American nation. As a leading revolutionary agitator against Britain for a decade after the Stamp Act crisis, Thomson was widely acclaimed as "the Sam. Adams of Phyladelphia— the Life of the Cause of Liberty." In his capacity as the first and only secretary of the Continental Congress during its fifteen-year history, he became such a familiar figure in America and Europe alike, simply because he attested almost all of Congress' published papers, that many Europeans reportedly believed that "Washington by his *Sword* and Secretary Thomson by his *Pen*" were primarily responsible for the achievement of American independence. And even twenty years after Thomson's retirement from public life in 1789 a reviewer of the aged patriot's monumental translation of the Bible felt that it was sufficient to identify the translator merely as "the venerable old man" who was "Secretary of Congress during the Revolution," well knowing that Thomson required no further introduction to an early nineteenth-century American audience.[1]

Yet despite the prominence he enjoyed during his lifetime, the relative obscurity into which Thomson sank after his death is not difficult to explain. As time passed and the American public began to downplay the revolutionary dimension of the struggle with Britain, popular interest in the statesmen, diplomats, and generals who conducted the War for Independence grew at the expense of radical leaders like Thomson who had spearheaded the opposition to British imperial policies before 1776. Furthermore, although Thomson was a central figure in the history of the Continental Congress, he occupied an ostensibly routine position that was never

---

[1] John Adams, Diary, August 30, 1774, Lyman H. Butterfield et al., eds., *Diary and Autobiography of John Adams*, 4 vols. (Cambridge, Mass., 1961), II, 115; Henry Peterson to Charles Thomson, June 21, 1783, Charles Thomson Papers, Vol. I, Library of Congress; *Monthly Anthology and Boston Review*, VII (1809), 396-400.

calculated to capture the popular imagination. But the most important reason for Thomson's posthumous public neglect is undoubtedly the decision he made sometime before his death to destroy most of his personal papers, for without them historians have found it extraordinarily difficult to reconstruct the details of his career or recapture the essense of his personality.[2] Therefore, in addition to shedding new light on a revealing episode in the life of the young American republic, the publication of the richly descriptive letters that he wrote to his second wife, Hannah Harrison Thomson, during Congress' brief sojourn at Princeton in 1783 will, we hope, also call attention to Thomson's superb gifts as a chronicler of the historic events in which he took part and suggest the enormity of the loss historical scholarship has suffered because of his failure to preserve the bulk of his private papers for posterity.

Charles Thomson's early life was like a tale from the pages of Horatio Alger. Born in County Derry, Ulster in November 1729, Thomson had an extremely unsettled youth. His mother, whose

---

[2] This does not mean, however, that Thomson has also failed to attract scholarly attention. Lewis R. Harley, *The Life of Charles Thomson* (Philadelphia, 1900); and J. Edwin Hendricks, *Charles Thomson and the Making of the New Nation, 1729-1824* (Cranbury, N. J., 1979), offer full-length biographies of Thomson. Lewis R. Harley, *Charles Thomson: Patriot and Scholar* (Norristown, Pa., 1897), 9-42; and J. Edwin Hendricks, "Charles Thomson and the Creation of 'A New Order of the Age,' " John Boles, ed., *America in the Middle Period: Essays in Honor of Bernard Mayo* (Charlottesville, Va., 1973), 1-13, provide convenient summaries of their longer works. Boyd Stanley Schlenther, "Training for Resistance: Charles Thomson and Indian Affairs in Pennsylvania," *Pennsylvania History*, L (1983), 185-217, deals insightfully with Thomson's relationship with the Friendly Association in Pennsylvania during the first half of the French and Indian War. John J. Zimmerman, "Charles Thomson, 'The Sam Adams of Philadelphia,' " *Mississippi Valley Historical Review*, XLV (1958), 464-80, describes Thomson's role as a revolutionary agitator in Philadelphia during the Stamp Act and Townshend crises. Jennings B. Sanders, *Evolution of the Executive Departments of the Continental Congress, 1774-1789* (Chapel Hill, N. C., 1935), Ch. X; and Frederick S. Rolater, "Charles Thomson, 'Prime Minister' of the United States," *Pennsylvania Magazine of History and Biography*, CI (1977), 322-48, cover Thomson's tenure as secretary of the Continental Congress. Kenneth R. Bowling, "Good-bye 'Charle': The Lee-Adams Interest and the Political Demise of Charles Thomson, Secretary of Congress, 1774-1789," *Pennsylvania Magazine of History and Biography*, C (1976), 314-35, analyzes the reasons for the abrupt termination of Thomson's political career in 1789. Albert J. Edmunds, "Charles

name has been lost to history, died a few years after his birth, and his father, John Thomson, a Presbyterian who was somehow involved in the linen trade, further disrupted the boy's life by immigrating to America in 1740 with Charles and three of his older brothers, leaving behind in Ireland a younger brother and sister. Unfortunately for Charles and his brothers, John Thomson died during the voyage to America, and the captain of the ship purloined most of the money with which the elder Thomson had hoped to make a fresh start in a new land. Orphaned and almost penniless upon their arrival at Newcastle, Delaware, Charles' older brothers set out to make their fortunes while leaving him with a local blacksmith and his family. But Thomson did not remain with this family for long. Upon learning that the blacksmith planned to have him bound as his apprentice, Thomson, who even then aspired to be more in life than just an artisan, immediately packed his clothes and ran away from home. Soon thereafter the young wanderer met an otherwise unidentified "gentlewoman" who lived nearby and who agreed to help him when he told her that he was eager to become a scholar.[3]

Thomson's fortuitous encounter with this mysterious benefactress proved to be an important turning point in his life. With her assistance he gained admission to an academy run by the Reverend Francis Alison in New London, Pennsylvania, where he was able to complete his studies thanks to the financial support he received from one of his brothers. Under the expert tutelage of Alison, a Presbyterian minister and graduate of the University of Edinburgh who was one of the most highly regarded pedagogues of the day, Thomson received a solid grounding in Greek and Latin, English

---

Thomson's New Testament," *Pennsylvania Magazine of History and Biography,* xv (1891), 327-35; and John F. Lyons, "Thomson's Bible," *Journal of the Presbyterian Historical Society,* xv (1938-39), 211-20, describe Thomson's contributions as a biblical translator. But the size of the scholarly literature on Thomson is somewhat deceptive. With the exception of the articles by Bowling and Schlenther, these works generally fail to probe beneath the surface of events and explain the deeper springs of Thomson's actions, an unfortunate byproduct of the loss of most of his personal papers.

[3] John F. Watson, "Biographical Memoir of the Hon. Charles Thomson, Secretary of the First Congress," *Collections of the Historical Society of Pennsylvania,* i (1853), 83-84. Watson's memoir is an especially valuable source because it is based on information he received first-hand from Thomson himself.

grammar and composition, belles-lettres, and natural and moral philosophy that was destined to be of great use to him in the years ahead. At the same time he began to demonstrate those habits of industry that were to make him such a successful secretary of the Continental Congress. On one occasion he walked from New London to Philadelphia and back in one day just to acquire a complete edition of the *Spectator*, whose style he greatly admired, and another time he journeyed by foot to Perth Amboy to consult with a British officer who was reputed to be highly proficient in Greek, a language the young scholar was still struggling to master. After graduating from Alison's academy, Thomson opened a subscription school for neighborhood children on a farm located near the boundary of Delaware and Pennsylvania and enjoyed great success as a teacher. But this was not enough to satisfy a young man who was fired by the conviction that as "the work of some intelligent Being . . . there must have been some design in bringing me into existence . . . [and] That end must be worthy the divine author."[4] Setting his sights higher, he moved to Philadelphia in 1750 and brought himself to the attention of Benjamin Franklin, who was so impressed by reports he had heard of Thomson's teaching skill that he arranged for him to be appointed as a tutor in Greek and Latin at the Academy of Philadelphia, the precursor of the University of Pennsylvania. This marked the beginning of a personal and political association between Franklin and Thomson that endured for four decades.[5]

It did not take long for Thomson to carve out a place for himself in Philadelphia society as a teacher, a champion of Indian rights, and a merchant. He taught classical languages at the Academy of Philadelphia from 1750 to 1755, and served for the next five years as a master of the Latin School at the Friends Public School in Philadelphia. His appointment to the latter position was a signal

[4] Charles Thomson, Memorandum Book, Historical Society of Pennsylvania, quoted in Hendricks, *Charles Thomson*, 10; Watson, "Biographical Memoir," 84; Lawrence A. Cremin, *American Education: The Colonial Experience, 1607-1783* (New York, 1970), 325.

[5] "American Biography," *American Quarterly Review,* I (1827), 30. This source contains many interesting biographical details about Thomson supplied by someone who is simply described as "one of his most intimate and accomplished friends." John F. Watson, the Philadelphia antiquarian, may have been the person in question.

achievement for the young Presbyterian, because the Public School normally required members of its faculty to be adherents of the Quaker religion. The exception made in Thomson's case undoubtedly stemmed from the fact that he openly sided with the Quakers in their dispute with the proprietor of Pennsylvania over the issue of Indian policy. Between 1756 and 1758 Thomson served as the agent of the Friendly Association, an organization of Quakers that eventually became dedicated to the proposition that proprietary mistreatment of the Indians justified the introduction of royal government to Pennsylvania. In particular, he represented the Association in its dealings with Teedyuscung, a rather equivocal Delaware chieftain whose complaints against the proprietor the Quaker organization hoped to use in its efforts to influence the imperial administration in England. He attended conferences between Pennsylvania government officials and Teedyuscung, serving as the Delaware chief's secretary, and he wrote a lengthy pamphlet bitterly attacking the proprietors of Pennsylvania past and present for their failure to prevent the Indians from being defrauded of their lands, debauched by rum, and cheated by white settlers and traders. In 1759 Benjamin Franklin arranged to have this pamphlet published in England under the title of *An Enquiry into the Causes of the Alienation of the Delaware and Shawanese from the British Interest.* Although Thomson and the Friendly Association failed to convince the imperial administration of the need for royal government in Pennsylvania, the Delawares nevertheless rewarded him for his activities on their behalf by making him an adopted member of their tribe and naming him Wegh-wu-law-mo-end—"the man who talks the truth."[6]

Unsuccessful as an advocate for the Delawares and apparently finding teaching an unrewarding line of work, Thomson resigned from the Friends Public School in 1760 and entered the mercantile profession. He began as an importer of dry goods, soon acquired an interest in an iron furnace in New Jersey, and branched out to become a rum distiller near the end of the decade. Thomson's transition from teacher to merchant was probably also influenced

[6] Watson, "Biographical Memoir," 90-91: Schlenther, "Training for Resistance," 185-206; Jean S. Straub, "Teaching in the Friends' Latin School of Philadelphia," *Pennsylvania Magazine of History and Biography,* XCI (1967), 434, 441.

by his marriage in 1758 to Ruth Mather, the daughter of a Pennsylvania merchant and Anglican vestryman, about whom little is known beyond the fact that she died in 1770 after having given birth to twin boys who lived but a few days at most. Four years later Thomson married Hannah Harrison, the daughter of a well-to-do Pennsylvania landholder, who was also related to the moderate Pennsylvania revolutionary leader, John Dickinson. Deeply religious, slightly irreverent toward her husband, far more interested in social life than he, and possessed of a fine sense of humor, Hannah Thomson, as the letters printed in this volume suggest, served as her husband's personal and political confidante during their thirty-three years of married life. Much to their regret, their marriage failed to produce any children.[7]

Thomson's success as a teacher and as a merchant in Philadelphia was more than overshadowed by his emergence as a radical opponent of British colonial policy after 1763. At the conclusion of the French and Indian War Thomson was an ardent Anglo-American patriot who rejoiced in the "prodigious growth and power of the British Empire" and looked forward to the time when the "British Colonies would overspread this immense territory added to the Crown of Britain, carrying with them the religion of Protestants, and the laws, customs, manners and language of the country from whence they sprung; while England placed at the head of the Empire superintended the whole, and by the wisdom of her councils prevented the jarring interests of the several inferior states, united their strength for the general good, and guarded them from the attacks of foreign powers."[8] The subsequent attenuation of his loyalty to the Empire resulted from the convergence of several different factors. British efforts in the wake of the war to restrict American trade and paper money adversely affected him economically and led him to question the justice of the entire mercantile system on the grounds that it enriched the people of Britain at the expense of those of America. The imperial administration's deci-

[7] Harley, *Life of Charles Thomson*, 187-95; Hendricks, *Charles Thomson*, 51, 55-58, 82; "Letters of Hannah Thomson, 1785-1788," *Pennsylvania Magazine of History and Biography*, xiv (1890), 28-40.

[8] Thomson to Benjamin Franklin, November 26, 1769, Leonard W. Labaree et al., eds., *The Papers of Benjamin Franklin* (New Haven, Conn., 1959-), xvi, 239-40. Thomson was writing retrospectively in the passage quoted above.

sion to station a large force of British regulars in the colonies awakened in him traditional Whig fears about the danger posed to liberty by standing armies. And the passage of the Stamp Act by Parliament in 1765, which threatened to deprive Americans of their hallowed rights as Englishmen to be taxed by their consent and tried by juries of their peers, crystallized his misgivings about British policy into the settled conviction that the government of Britain was engaged in nothing less than a systematic conspiracy to destroy American liberties. "There is a regular system laid down to govern America by absolute authority," he wrote in his private memorandum book at the time of the Stamp Act crisis. "What liberty can that people enjoy whose will is subjected to the absolute will of another, under the notion of regulating it."[9]

Thomson's conviction that the British government was conspiring against American liberty—a conspiracy for which he long absolved the king of any responsibility—drove him to political action. Abandoning his previous fondness for royal government, he joined with other Philadelphia merchants in mobilizing popular support to nullify the enforcement of the Stamp Act in Pennsylvania and advocated the adoption of non-importation agreements to compel Parliament to repeal the obnoxious law. He also wrote strongly worded letters to Benjamin Franklin and his mercantile correspondents in England explaining why Americans regarded Parliament's attempt to tax them as a fundamental threat to the security of their liberty and property, two of which were published by Franklin in London newspapers to persuade the British of the futility of trying to impose this unpopular measure on America. Thomson rejoiced when Parliament repealed the Stamp Act, significantly noting that as a result of this action "our love and allegiance to our King is entire and unshaken,"[10] but he was filled with new foreboding when it passed the Townshend Acts in 1767. In the face

[9] Charles Thomson, Memorandum Book, Historical Society of Pennsylvania, quoted in Schlenther, "Training for Resistance," 217n.103. See also Thomson to A Correspondent in London, June 24, 1765, Labaree et al., eds., *Franklin Papers*, xii, 183-85; Same to Benjamin Franklin, [September 24, 1765], *ibid.*, 278-80; Same to Welsh, Wilkinson & Co., November 7, 1765, "Thomson Papers," New-York Historical Society, *Collections*, xi (1878), 5-6; and Same to Cook, Lawrence & Co., November 9, 1765, *ibid.*, 8-12.

[10] Thomson to Benjamin Franklin, May 20, 1766, Labaree et al., eds., *Franklin Papers*, xiii, 278-79. In addition to the letters cited in note 9, see also Hendricks,

of this latest parliamentary effort to tax the colonies, Thomson worked even harder than before to defend American liberties against perceived British threats. Joining with John Dickinson, the celebrated Pennsylvania Farmer, he wrote newspaper essays, lobbied with his fellow merchants, and organized and addressed mass meetings to win popular approval for a program of non-importation of British goods that was designed to force Parliament to rescind the new duties. Moreover, when the merchants began to turn against non-importation after Parliament repealed all but one of the Townshend duties in 1770, Thomson, who feared that the retention of the duty on tea was but the prelude to further parliamentary taxation, mobilized the artisans, craftsmen, and mechanics of Philadelphia to keep the merchants in line. In thus reaching out to social groups which had traditionally played a largely passive role in Pennsylvania politics Thomson failed to prevent the collapse of the non-importation movement in the province, but in the process he nevertheless managed to solidify his position as the boldest opponent of imperial policy in Philadelphia and lay the groundwork for the formation of an even more radical resistance group in that city during the climax of the revolutionary crisis between America and Britain.[11]

The deceptive lull that settled over Anglo-American relations in the aftermath of the Townshend crisis was soon shattered by a series of events that turned Thomson from an advocate of resistance to a supporter of revolution against Britain. Parliament's passage of the Tea Act in 1773 reconfirmed his belief in the existence of a British conspiracy to subvert American liberties and led him to contemplate for the first time the possibility that the colonies might have to take up arms to vindicate their rights against the encroachments of the mother country. Even at this late date, however, he hoped that any military conflict would ultimately lead to the creation of a constitutional union between America and Britain

---

Charles Thomson, Ch. III; and Zimmerman, "Charles Thomson, 'The Sam Adams of Philadelphia,' " 467-71.

[11] Thomson to Benjamin Franklin, November 26, 1769, Labaree et al., eds., *Franklin Papers*, XVI, 237-40; Hendricks, *Charles Thomson*, Ch. IV; Zimmerman, "Charles Thomson, 'The Sam Adams of Philadelphia,' " 472-79; Richard Alan Ryerson, *The Revolution Is Now Begun: The Radical Committees of Philadelphia, 1765-1776* (Philadelphia, 1978), 28-32.

specifically defining the rights and responsibilities of each within the framework of the Empire. Though this hope grew dim in the following year when Parliament responded to the Boston Tea Party by approving the Coercive Acts, Thomson continued to work for reform within the Empire. He played a key role in arousing popular support in Pennsylvania for a meeting of delegates from all the colonies to seek redress of American grievances from Britain, and he backed the ensuing Continental Congress' policy of employing economic coercion and direct appeals to the king and people of Britain to bring about the reorganization of the Empire along federal lines. Britain's studied refusal to accede to the terms Congress laid down for Anglo-American reconciliation and the outbreak of armed conflict at Lexington and Concord blasted Thomson's hopes for a peaceful resolution of the imperial crisis. But it was the king's rejection of the Olive Branch Petition, which was tendered to him by Congress in the summer of 1775, which finally convinced Thomson that American liberties could not be safe, nor American property secure, in an empire based on the principle of virtually unlimited parliamentary authority over the colonies and ruled by a monarch who was insensitive to American rights and interests. Thus by the end of 1775 Thomson was completely transformed from an Anglo-American subject who gloried in being a member of the British Empire to an American patriot who favored the formation of an independent confederation of the colonies. Still, the mere fact that this transformation took twelve years to complete eloquently attests to the strength of the ties of imperial loyalty that had once bound him to Britain.[12]

Thomson's prominence in the Philadelphia revolutionary movement led to his appointment to the office for which he is best remembered in American history. The First Continental Congress, which was then meeting in the Quaker City, offered him the post of secretary of Congress on September 5, 1774, and Thomson, whose conservative political opponents in Pennsylvania had pre-

[12] The best source for reconstructing Thomson's political evolution between 1773 and 1775 is Thomson to William Henry Drayton, [1778-1779], *Pennsylvania Magazine of History and Biography*, ii (1878), 411-23, a defense of John Dickinson's conduct during that phase of the American Revolution which reveals much about Thomson as well. See also Merrill M. Jensen, *The Founding of a Nation: A History of the American Revolution, 1763-1776* (New York, 1968), 443; and Hendricks, *Charles Thomson*, Ch. vi.

vented him from becoming a regular member of that august body, readily agreed to accept it.[13] Thomson initially expected his tenure to be brief, but in fact he held this position until the Continental Congress itself was superseded fifteen years later by the new system of government created by the Federal Constitution. In the meantime, however, he became one of the few elements of stability in the Old Congress' often turbulent history. For, far from being a mere clerk, Thomson in his capacity as secretary of Congress was entrusted with wide-ranging responsibilities that were vital to the effective conduct of congressional business. By performing these manifold duties with such obvious efficiency and undeniable zeal for the national interest, he became the most indispensible civil servant of all to the Congress that united thirteen colonies in opposition to Great Britain, forged the Articles of Confederation, organized the western territories acquired during the peace negotiations with Britain, and maintained at least a semblance of national authority during the difficult postwar years of readjustment.

At first Thomson's primary secretarial responsibilities consisted of keeping a record of Congress' proceedings and preserving its archives. Thus, except for rare occasions when he was ill or away on leave, Thomson attended every meeting of Congress and took rough notes of the business it transacted. He then entered a more polished version of these notes in one of three journals he regularly kept. The first of these, the Rough Journal, contained records of congressional actions that were generally deemed suitable for publication, whereas the other two, the Secret Domestic Journal and the Secret Journal of Foreign Affairs, consisted of records of congressional proceedings that were considered too sensitive for public disclosure. Thomson followed one rule in compiling these journals that has been a source of deep regret to all students of the American Revolution. In an effort to lighten his burden of work and at the same time create an impression of national unity in Congress, he systematically excluded all speeches delivered by members of Congress as well as all motions that failed to win congressional approval. Fortunately, he preserved manuscript texts

[13] Paul H. Smith et al., eds., *Letters of Delegates to Congress, 1774-1789* (Washington, D. C., 1976-), I, 10, 12n.8, 20-23.

of many of the defeated motions in the archives of Congress. But if Thomson is open to criticism for failing to include important matter in the journals of Congress, he deserves nothing but praise for the care with which he organized and maintained the immense number of documents generated and received by that body. The more than 50,000 surviving papers of the Continental Congress now in the custody of the National Archives—many of them bearing Thomson's careful docketings—offer perhaps the best evidence of his archival skills as well as his concern to preserve a crucial part of the documentary history of the American Revolution for posterity.[14]

Thomson's duties as secretary were not confined to keeping a record of Congress' deliberations and taking care of its papers. In recognition of his unflagging industry and untiring devotion to public service, Congress assigned many other responsibilities to him as well, only the most important of which need be mentioned here. Thomson helped to supervise the publication of the journals and state papers of Congress, and successfully insisted that Congress render a truthful account of current events in its periodic communications to the public on the progress of the war. He kept the Great Seal of the United States and affixed it to all acts of Congress. He served as a liaison between Congress and its executive departments, and monitored state compliance with congressional recommendations. He issued letters of marque and passports, attested military commissions, and oversaw the removal of the records of Congress during its various peregrinations in war and peace. And from time to time he submitted reports to Congress, advised the members thereof on matters of public policy, corresponded with American diplomats overseas, translated foreign dispatches, and presided over Congress during the interval between the retirement of one president and the election of another.[15] Thomson's length

[14] "American Biography," *American Quarterly Review*, I (1827), 31; Herbert Friedenwald, "The Journals and Papers of the Continental Congress," American Historical Association, *Annual Report*, I (1896), 85-127.

[15] Sanders, *Evolution of the Executive Departments*, Ch. x; Rolater, "Charles Thomson, 'Prime Minister' of the United States," 322-48. Rolater's article must be used with care. It is riddled with basic factual errors, and its effort to compare the office of secretary of the Continental Congress to that of a British prime minister is seriously flawed by the simple fact that Thomson had neither a personal nor a party following in Congress.

of service as secretary and the wide variety of duties he performed made him a key figure in the history of the Continental Congress, as a minor French diplomat who knew him well explained in 1785:

> Mr. Thomson is the oldest servant of congress, and there has been no one more constant in all the revolutions which have agitated this assembly. He is a man wise, uniform, and full of moderation. The confidence of congress in him has no limits, and, although he has not the right to speak in the debates of this assembly, he has often been consulted, because he has been present for the last ten years at everything which took place there, and he can contribute to maintain a uniform system better than the delegates who are continually changing, and who sometimes know nothing of the doings of their predecessors.[16]

In the end Thomson was ill-requited for his decade and a half of service to the nation. After the Articles of Confederation were replaced by the Constitution of 1787, he was rebuffed in his efforts to serve the new federal government either as secretary of the Senate or as head of a projected Home Department, the functions of which would have closely resembled the ones he performed as secretary of the Continental Congress. Instead, the Senate selected Samuel Allyne Otis of Massachusetts as its clerk, and Congress assigned the duties of the Home Office to the newly created Department of State. In addition, the committee in charge of planning George Washington's first inauguration ceremony conspicuously omitted Thomson from the list of invited guests—and this despite the fact that it was none other than Thomson himself who had brought the official news of Washington's election to Mount Vernon! The harsh treatment Thomson received in 1789 was in part the work of some former members of the Continental Congress whom he had offended during his tenure as secretary, most notably adherents of the fabled Lee-Adams interest who believed that he had worked against them during the bitter dispute between Silas Deane and Arthur Lee that had sharply divided Congress a decade before. But there was a deeper reason for the rejection of Thom-

---

[16] Barbé-Marbois to Comte de Vergennes, February 25, 1785, George Bancroft, *History of the Formation of the Constitution of the United States*, 2 vols. (2d ed., New York, 1882), i, 414.

son's attempts to obtain a federal office. By virtue of his lengthy tenure as secretary of the Continental Congress, Thomson had become a living symbol of the very system of government whose weaknesses had brought about the constitutional revolution of 1787, and even though he had personally favored reform of the Articles of Confederation, he still remained a vivid reminder of a period of American history that the triumphant Federalists who dominated the Washington administration were determined to repudiate once and for all. Thus, keenly disappointed by his inability to continue in public service, Thomson retired to private life in the summer of 1789, comforted at the last moment by a letter from Washington reminding him "that your Services have been important, as your patriotism was distinguished" and urging him to "enjoy that best of all rewards, the consciousness of having done your duty well."[17]

Thomson spent thirty-five years of retirement at "Harriton," a small estate just outside of Philadelphia inherited by his wife Hannah. These years were marked by one great tragedy and one great triumph. The first involved the loss of his history of the American Revolution. In view of his activities as a revolutionary leader in Philadelphia and his unsurpassed knowledge of the inner workings of the Continental Congress, Thomson was frequently urged to write a historical account of the Revolution. "When I consider that no person in the world is so perfectly acquainted with the rise, conduct and conclusion of the American Revolution as yourself," John Jay once wrote to him, expressing the opinion of many, "I cannot but wish that you would devote one hour in the four and twenty to giving Posterity a true account of it."[18] And indeed Thomson did try to discharge this obligation to posterity. In 1785 he informed a French diplomat that he had written a thousand folio pages of "secret historical memoirs" describing everything he had left out of the journals of Congress, and near the end of his life he confided to a friend in Pennsylvania that he had continued to work on this manuscript after his retirement from public life in

[17] George Washington to Thomson, July 24, 1789, John C. Fitzpatrick, ed., *The Writings of George Washington*, 39 vols. (Washington, D. C., 1931-1944), xxx, 359; Bowling, "Good-by 'Charle,' " 314-35.

[18] John Jay to Thomson, July 19, 1783, "Thomson Papers," New-York Historical Society, *Collections*, xi (1878), 174-75.

1789. But, alas, at some point early in the 1790s he decided that publication of his history would be contrary to the best interests of the new American nation, and so he destroyed the precious manuscript. "No, no . . . I will not," he replied to a subsequent request that he compose a history of the Revolution. "I could not tell the truth without giving great offense. Let the world admire our patriots and heroes. Their supposed talents and virtues (where they were so) by commanding imitation will serve the cause of patriotism and our country."[19] In Thomson's opinion, then, it was more important to nurture the growth of American nationalism by fostering a heroic legend of the Founding Fathers than to provide posterity with an accurate account of the divisions among them that had attended the birth of the nation. Thomson's decision to destroy his history is even more regrettable because he left behind two lengthy descriptions of Pennsylvania politics during the critical years of 1774-1775 which reveal that he possessed a rare talent for vivid personal characterization and shrewd historical analysis.[20]

The tragic destruction of Thomson's history of the Revolution was offset by his triumphant translation of the Bible. Thomson's decision to devote almost the first two decades of his retirement to the demanding task of biblical translation stemmed from his personal religious needs. Though he was born and bred a Presbyterian and belonged to the First Presbyterian Church of Philadelphia for more than a quarter of a century before his withdrawal from public affairs, Thomson was at heart a Christian rationalist whose reason led him to believe "only in the Scriptures, and in Jesus Christ, my Saviour."[21] Yet although Thomson accepted the Bible as "a book containing the immediate revelation of God's will to man,"[22] he was

[19] Benjamin Rush to John Adams, February 12, 1812, Lyman H. Butterfield, ed., *The Letters of Benjamin Rush*, 2 vols. (Princeton, 1951), ii, 1123. See also Barbé-Marbois to Comte de Vergennes, February 25, 1785, Bancroft, *History of the Constitution*, i, 414; Watson, "Biographical Memoir," 91; and George W. Corner, ed., *The Autobiography of Benjamin Rush* (Princeton, 1948), 155.

[20] Thomson to William Henry Drayton, [1778-1779], *Pennsylvania Magazine of History and Biography*, ii (1878), 411-23; Same to David Ramsay, November 4, 1786, Paul H. Smith, ed., "Charles Thomson on Unity in the American Revolution," *Quarterly Journal of the Library of Congress*, xxviii (1971), 158-72.

[21] Corner, ed., *Autobiography of Benjamin Rush*, 294.

[22] Thomson to Samuel Miller, January 6, 1801, Charles Thomson Papers, Vol. iii, Library of Congress.

deeply troubled by two Deistic criticisms of sacred scripture. The first was that Jesus Christ did not fulfill the prophecies of the Old Testament, and the second was that the four Evangelists were internally inconsistent and therefore not divinely inspired. In reaction to the first line of criticism, Thomson carefully studied the Septuagint, the famous pre-Christian Greek rendition of the Hebrew Old Testament, and concluded that Jesus had in fact fulfilled the Old Testament prophecies. To prove this point beyond all doubt, he prepared the first translation of the Septuagint from Greek into English and retranslated the New Testament as well, striving throughout to "give a just and true representation of the sense & meaning of the sacred scriptures and . . . to convey into the translation as far as I could the Spirit & manner of the authors and thereby give it the quality of the Original, making it appear natural & easy, using no words improperly, or in a meaning unwarranted by use, and combining them in a way so as not to render the sense obscure and the construction harsh or ungrammatical."[23] The resultant work, printed in four volumes in Philadelphia in 1808, was entitled *The Holy Bible, Containing the Old and New Covenant, Commonly Called the Old and the New Testament*. Criticized by some contemporaries for being too literal in its rendering of the text, Thomson's translation has also been praised by a modern authority for its "clearness, force and felicitous language."[24] Then, in order to refute criticism that the Evangelists were inconsistent in their treatment of the events of Jesus' life, he immediately began work on a harmony of the Gospels. This volume, published in Philadelphia in 1815 as *A Synopsis of the Four Evangelists*, consisted of related passages from Thomson's translation of the Gospels arranged in parallel columns and triumphantly proclaimed that even though "infidels still continue to charge the Evangelists with inconsistency and contradiction . . . on a full and fair examination, it will be found that the Evangelists are neither inconsistent, nor

[23] *Ibid.*
[24] John Davis to Ebenezer Hazard, April 29, 1809, Paul O. Clark, ed., "Letters of Charles Thomson on the Translation of the Bible," *Journal of the Presbyterian Historical Society*, xxxiv (1956), 118; *Monthly Anthology and Boston Review,* viii (1810), 197-98; P. Marion Simms, *The Bible in America* (New York, 1936), 145. See also Albert J. Edmunds, "Charles Thomson's New Testament," 327-35; and John F. Lyons, "Thomson's Bible," 211-20.

do they contradict one another; but that, on the contrary, they mutually elucidate, support, and confirm one another's narration."[25] And with the completion of this book Thomson's active life came to an end, for shortly after its publication he suffered a debilitating series of illnesses and began to lapse into senility.

When Thomson died in his ninety-fifth year on August 16, 1824, the nation correctly mourned the passing of one of its founders. "Farewell thou hoary headed patriot and sage!" one Pennsylvania newspaper typically intoned. "A great nation will truly feel thy loss."[26] But perhaps the most revealing tribute to the deceased patriot was paid three years afterwards by an unidentified friend, who remembered him as follows:

> His conversation before his mind had bent beneath the pressure of years, was a rich fund of information and entertainment on these subjects [the American Revolution]. His natural temper was remarkably good and cheerful, and nothing delighted him more than free and social conversation with his friends: he possessed a great share of natural sagacity; he seemed to penetrate into the characters of men, and into their motives, with surprising facility; and he could, when provoked, or the occasion called for it, use a caustic severity in reproof, which was felt the more severely, as not inflicted willingly. He was a true republican of the old school; he hated all the "necessities" of royalty, and the pomp and trappings of aristocracy. He was most strictly moral and religious, attending more to the spirit than to the forms of religion, but his mind was fully imbued with the great truths of Christianity.[27]

[25] Thomson, *A Synopsis of the Evangelists* (Philadelphia, 1815), iii-iv. Thomas Jefferson praised the *Synopsis* as a "work [which] bears the stamp of that accuracy which marks every thing from you, and will be useful to those who, not taking things on trust, recur for themselves to the pure fountain of morals." Jefferson to Thomson, January 9, 1816, Dickinson W. Adams, ed., *Jefferson's Extracts from the Gospels* (Princeton, 1983), 364.

[26] *Norristown Herald*, August 25, 1824, quoted in "Obituary Notices of Pennsylvania Soldiers of the American Revolution," *Pennsylvania Magazine of History and Biography*, xxxviii (1914), 454-55.

[27] "American Biography," *American Quarterly Review*, i (1827), 31.

Just as some background on Charles Thomson is necessary to appreciate his letters, so is some understanding of the history and problems of the Congress of the United States. As the only secretary of that organization, Thomson watched these difficulties evolve at close hand and probably knew more about the inner history of the institution than any other person.

His encyclopedic knowledge was not always a comfort. As these letters make clear, he believed that Congress was in deep trouble by 1783, and he was not at all sure that the United States could survive this ordeal intact. At the moment of the republic's greatest triumph while everyone awaited news of the signing of the definitive peace treaty establishing the independence of the United States, Congress fled from angry soldiers in Philadelphia and established itself in the unincorporated village of Princeton, New Jersey. Jammed into uncomfortable quarters in hot and unpleasant weather, the members struggled merely to get and maintain a quorum for ordinary business. More quietly, some of them, including Thomson, worried whether the new nation could hold together without the war and an active British menace as inducements to union. Had the republic secured its independence only to dissolve into two or three separate confederacies? How had such a crisis come about?

Like the republic it served, Congress had always been an improvisation. The First Continental Congress began in 1774 as a protest movement, a means of expressing the united opposition of the mainland colonies to Britian's Coercive Acts, which in turn were the mother country's retribution for the Boston Tea Party of December 1773. When the Second Continental Congress met in May 1775, it already had a war on its hands, for fighting had broken out a few weeks earlier at Lexington and Concord. Somewhat reluctantly, Congress took charge of this effort and in the process found itself becoming a government—almost. It created the Continental Army and Navy, printed paper money worth millions of dollars, took over the post office, coordinated the resistance movements throughout the continent, and served as an arbiter of the legitimacy of the ad hoc governments in particular provinces. After independence, it moved to establish diplomatic relations with foreign nations. Only then did it begin in a serious way to define its own powers. The Articles of Confederation, discussed at various points in the seventeen months after independence, were not finally

By His EXCELLENCY

Elias Boudinot, Esquire,

President of the United States in Congress Assembled.

A PROCLAMATION.

WHEREAS a body of armed Soldiers in the service of the United States, and quartered in the Barracks of this City, having mutinously renounced their obedience to their Officers, did, on Saturday the Twenty-First Day of this instant, proceed, under the direction of their Serjeants, in a hostile and threatning manner, to the Place in which Congress were assembled, and did surround the same with Guards: And whereas Congress in consequence thereof, did on the same Day, resolve, " That the President and Supreme Executive Council of this State " should be informed, that the authority of the United States having been, that Day, grossly insulted by the " disorderly and menacing appearance of a body of armed Soldiers, about the Place within which Congress were assem- " bled; and that the Peace of this City being endangered by the mutinous Disposition of the said Troops then in the " Barracks; it was, in the Opinion of Congress, necessary, that effectual Measures should be immediately taken for " supporting the public Authority:" And also whereas Congress did at the same Time appoint a Committee to con-fer with the said President and Supreme Executive Council on the practicability of carrying the said Resolution in o due effect: And also whereas the said Committee have reported to me, that they have not received satisfactory Assurances for expecting adequate and prompt exertions of this State for supporting the Dignity of the fœderal Government: And also whereas the said Soldiers still continue in a state of open Mutiny and Revolt, so that the Dignity and Authority of the United States would be constantly exposed to a repetition of Insult, while Congress shall continue to sit in this City, . I do therefore, by and with the Advice of the said Committee, and according to the Powers and Authorities in me vest-ed for this Purpose, hereby summon the honourable the Delegates composing the Congress of the United States, and every of them, to meet in Congress on Thursday the Twenty Sixth Day of June instant, at Princeton, in the state of New-Jersey, in order that further and more effectual Measures may be taken for suppressing the present Revolt, and maintaining the Dignity and Authority of the United States, of which all Officers of the United States, civil and military, and all others whom it may concern, are desired to take Notice and govern themselves accordingly.

GIVEN under my Hand and Seal at Philadelphia, in the state of Pennsylvania, this Twenty-Fourth Day of June, in the Year of Our Lord One Thousand Seven Hundred and Eighty-Three, and of the Sovereignty and Inde-pendence the seventh.

ELIAS BOUDINOT.

Attest.

SAMUEL STERETT, Private Secretary.

Proclamation by Elias Boudinot, President of the Continental Congress,
summoning that body to meet at Princeton, New Jersey,
printed in Philadelphia by David C. Claypoole, June 24, 1783
Princeton University Library

approved by Congress until November 1777. The states then took nearly three and one-half years to ratify the document. By March 1781 when the Articles finally went into effect, the pressures of war had already forced major changes in the way that Congress conducted business, especially in the movement toward the creation of executive departments. Events always had a way of outdistancing the ability of Congress to control or respond to them. Probably at no time did members of Congress believe that, as a body, they were adequate to their tasks. Other than the loyalists, the severest critics of Congress were often its own members.[28]

Thus Congress became what it was through a series of pragmatic or ad hoc decisions. Each of these choices made good political sense in the context in which it arose, but the combined effect of all of them—the momentum generated by the process as a whole—successively narrowed the authority of the United States over time. Congress was a more powerful body in 1775 and 1776 than in 1781 or 1783. Many delegates contributed willingly to a process whose net result most of them learned to lament. How this happened requires a closer look at some details.

From its first session in 1774, Congress voted by colony, not by individual delegates. Men sitting for large provinces favored proportional representation from the start, but they lost. Adequate population data had not been compiled for most colonies by 1774. Without proper statistics, who could say what proportions should prevail?[29] Provincial (or later, state) equality became a simple solution to a real problem, and hard political considerations reinforced this conclusion. Support for the Revolution tended to be weaker in many small colonies than in most of the large ones. New Jersey, Delaware, Maryland and Georgia had to be coaxed toward independence, as did New York.[30] A strident insistence on pro-

---

[28] See generally Jensen, *The Founding of a Nation*; David Ammerman, *In the Common Cause: American Response to the Coercive Acts of 1774* (Charlottesville, Va., 1974); H. James Henderson, *Party Politics in the Continental Congress* (New York, 1974); Jack N. Rakove, *The Beginnings of National Politics: An Interpretive History of the Continental Congress* (New York, 1979); and Arnold M. Pavlovsky, " 'Between Hawk and Buzzard': Congress as Perceived by its Members, 1775-1783," *Pennsylvania Magazine of History and Biography*, CI (1977), 349-64.

[29] James Duane's Notes of Debates, September 6, 1774, in Smith et al., eds., *Letters of Delegates to Congress*, I, 30-31.

[30] John A. Neuenschwander, *The Middle Colonies and the Coming of the American*

portional representation might have alienated some of these provinces sufficiently to drive them back into British arms, a possibility that patriots dreaded as an utter catastrophe. A serious break in colonial unity could have destroyed the Revolution. This principle had a corollary that contemporaries refrained from expressing quite as clearly. So long as the British Empire offered a viable alternative to a continental union, the tail could wag the dog in North America.

The drafters of formal proposals of American union took about a year to absorb this lesson. The two earliest plans prepared for Congress, by Benjamin Franklin of Pennsylvania and Silas Deane of Connecticut, both contained conspicuous nationalizing features. Franklin's, which he presented informally in July 1775, rested upon proportional representation, including amendment by a simple majority of states. He gave Congress broad powers over war and peace, foreign affairs, the regulation of trade, intercolonial disputes, and Indian relations. He even authorized Congress to make such laws as, "tho' necessary to the General Welfare, particular Assemblies cannot be competent to." Even though he permitted each colony to retain "as much as it may think fit of its own present Laws, Customs, Rights, Privileges, and peculiar jurisdictions within its own Limits," his broad allocation of authority to an incipient American union might conceivably have looked more like the later French Revolutionary nation in arms than an American federal relationship, except for two features. He gave Congress no power of taxation. And although his plan projected a "perpetual" union, it also provided for its liquidation should Britain meet America's stringent terms for reconciliation.[31]

Deane also proposed a permanent union, a "General Congress" to meet "at least once Annually forever." His plan in a rather cumbersome way anticipated the Federal Constitution's solution to the tensions between large and small states. Instead of a bicameral legislature in which one house represented people and the other states, he suggested that on some questions a majority of delegates

Revolution (Port Washington, N. Y., 1973); Ronald Hoffman, *A Spirit of Dissension: Economics, Politics and the Revolution in Maryland* (Baltimore, 1973); Kenneth Coleman, *Georgia in the American Revolution, 1763-1789* (Athens, Ga., 1958).

[31] Labaree et al., eds., *Franklin Papers*, XXII, 120-25, The quotations are from pp. 123 and 122.

should carry the day, while other motions would require a majority of both delegates and states. Congress would have the power "of laying any Duty, excise, or Custom on any Wares, or Merchandize," could choose governors to serve during good behavior (i.e., virtually for life) in any colony that had been governed directly by the crown, and could negative the laws of any colony in which the governor had possessed a veto. Deane's own colony of Connecticut, which had elective governors without a veto power, would have conveniently escaped the last two restrictions.[32]

Although still another Connecticut plan appeared in a Philadelphia newspaper in early 1776,[33] Congress did not turn seriously to the problem of confederation until the summer of that year. This time John Dickinson of Pennsylvania provided most of the leadership. American historians of widely divergent points of view have read the Dickinson plan as centralizing and nationalistic. Merrill Jensen (a Progressive with Antifederalist sympathies), W. W. Crosskey (an extreme nationalist with no tolerance for any other viewpoint), Winton U. Solberg (a moderate close to the mainstream of historical interpretation), and Jack Rakove (a moderate who denies that factional labels can explain much of anything about congressional politics) all agree that Dickinson tried to create some sort of consolidated republic.[34]

At best, the evidence for this claim is highly ambiguous. Dickinson's plan was manifestly less centralizing than either Franklin's or Deane's. He probably did prefer proportional representation to state equality. His early draft ignores the question, but the version reported to Congress affirms state equality, doubtless reflecting amendments made within his committee. He gave Congress no power to raise taxes or regulate commerce. Instead of Franklin's "General Welfare" clause, he gave to each state the exclusive control "of its internal Police, in all Matters that shall not interfere with

[32] Smith et al., eds., *Letters of Delegates to Congress*, II, 418-20.
[33] *The Pennsylvania Evening Post*, March 5, 1776.
[34] Merrill Jensen, *The Articles of Confederation: An Interpretation of the Social-Constitutional History of the American Revolution* (Madison, Wis., 1940), Ch. v; William Winslow Crosskey and William Jeffrey, Jr., *Politics and the Constitution in the History of the United States, III: The Political Background of the Federal Convention* (Chicago, 1980), Ch. vi; Winton U. Solberg, ed., *The Federal Convention and the Formation of the Union of the American States* (New York, 1958), 41; Rakove, *The Beginnings of National Politics*, 151-58.

the Articles of this Confederation." Ordinary measures would require the approval, not of a majority of states present, but of seven states. Important matters needed the votes of nine states, and amendments to the Articles would have to be approved by all of them. To be sure, Dickinson did enumerate the powers of Congress in greater detail than did any of the other early plans, but this effort probably aimed at limiting Congress, not freeing it from restraint. The Dickinson plan in either of its surviving drafts is far closer to the final Articles of Confederation than to either the Franklin or the Deane plans.[35]

The implications of this argument are fairly significant. The association between nationalist (or centralizer) and conservative on the one hand, and decentralizer and radical on the other hand, is quite venerable in the historiography of the Revolution, and it can indeed account for much of the political infighting between 1774 and 1790, especially at the constituency level. But it explains little about the specific process of drafting and ratifying the Articles of Confederation. Too many individuals somehow escaped these categories. Franklin, strongly linked with the radicals by 1775, nevertheless produced a centralizing plan. Thomas Paine, one of the most radical men in America in 1776, thought similarly on this question.[36] Deane, much more conservative than Franklin, does illustrate the stereotype in his support for a powerful union. But Dickinson, who was conservative enough to reject the Declaration of Independence without quite embracing loyalism, nevertheless drafted a plan of confederation that favored a more decentralized structure than anyone else had yet proposed. All it took to make this emphasis explicit was an amendment by Thomas Burke of North Carolina in 1777, eventually incorporated as Article II of the completed Articles of Confederation. Burke's proposal, inspired by a deep distrust of central authority, explicitly endorsed state sovereignty. "Each state," it declared, "retains its sovereignty, freedom and independence, and every power, jurisdiction, and right, which is not by this confederation expressly delegated to the

[35] See the two drafts of the Dickinson Plan, presented in parallel texts, in Smith et al., eds., *Letters of Delegates to Congress,* IV, 233-55. The quotation is from p. 234.

[36] Thomas Paine, *Common Sense* (1776), in Merrill Jensen, ed., *Tracts of the American Revolution, 1763-1776* (Indianapolis, 1967), 432.

United States in Congress assembled." At this stage of his career, Burke was a genuine radical, who thus matches the other half of the stereotype equating radicals with decentralization. Franklin, Deane, Dickinson and Burke cover, in short, every major patriot permutation of the period: radical nationalist, conservative nationalist, conservative localist, and radical localist. Nevertheless the drift over time is unmistakable—toward localism and states rights.[37]

The political dynamics of a rapidly shifting revolutionary situation help to explain this process. In the summer of 1775, the Franklin plan had to strike many delegates as a final affront to Britain, perhaps an insuperable barrier to the imperial reconciliation still sought by most delegates. The "perpetual" union announced in its title mocked the conciliation that its first article seemed to encourage, possibly as an afterthought. Accordingly, such radicals as John and Samuel Adams of Massachusetts or Richard Henry Lee and Thomas Jefferson of Virginia found it attractive. As of June 1776, by contrast, Dickinson believed that any final break with Britain would be suicidal unless the colonies had already established a firm union among themselves. His plea for confederation appealed to middle-colony conservatives who feared independence and hoped that the issue of confederation might provide a lever for postponing it.[38]

Congress did the opposite. It embraced independence before deciding the question of formal confederation. It certainly did have other things to worry about throughout the last half of 1776. Almost at the very moment that Congress declared independence in Philadelphia, the British began their massive invasion of New York when they landed unopposed on Staten Island on July 3. By December they had overrun Long Island, Manhattan, parts of Westchester, Newport, and New Jersey as far south as Burlington. Devastated by one overwhelming blow after another, the Continental Army nearly disintegrated. Its remnants fled across New Jersey and at last found temporary safety on the west bank of the Delaware. Thousands of men in New York and New Jersey swore allegiance to the crown, including even Richard Stockton, a member

[37] Thomas Burke to Richard Caswell, April 29, 1777, Smith et al., eds., *Letters of Delegates to Congress*, vi, 672; Solberg, ed., *The Federal Convention*, 42.

[38] See generally Jack N. Rakove, "The Decision for American Independence: A Reconstruction," *Perspectives in American History*, x (1976), 217-75.

of the first graduating class of the College of New Jersey, a trustee of the college, a leading figure in New Jersey's patriot movement, and a signer of the Declaration.[39] Such conservative patriots as New York's General Philip Schuyler and Maryland's Charles Carroll of Carrollton believed that North Americans should settle for the best terms they could get from the British, which obviously would not include independence.[40] Even Jefferson ruefully concluded as early as August 1776 that true patriots should start to make what we would call contingency plans to cover the possibility of a royal restoration.[41]

Washington's stunning victories at Trenton on December 26, 1776 and at Princeton eight days later reversed this momentum and gave the Revolution time to regroup. Although Britain's Hessian allies lost a thousand men at Trenton, that defeat was not irreparable. Charles Lord Cornwallis, Britain's best field commander in the American war, marched south determined, as he put it, to "bag the fox." He caught Washington at Trenton with his back to the Delaware late on the afternoon of January 2. Instead of trying to recross the river as Cornwallis expected, Washington stole past his adversary's open left flank and, after marching all night, mauled the British garrison at Princeton the next morning. That engagement, small as it was, produced huge results. Rather than pursue and destroy Washington's tattered army, the British took serious alarm, called in all of their outlying garrisons, and consolidated their position along the Raritan from New Brunswick to the sea. Politically, this decision abandoned most of New Jersey to the patriots, who now returned breathing vengeance upon those who had accepted British protection. As a revolutionary war, the military struggle was at root a battle for loyalties, a contest for the minds and hearts of the civilian population. At that level, Washington's two small victories really did offset General Sir William Howe's much bigger ones. It became obvious during the 1777 campaign for Philadelphia that the settlers would henceforth be far

[39] On Stockton, see James McLachlan, *Princetonians, 1748-1768: A Biographical Dictionary* (Princeton, 1976), 7-11.

[40] For Schuyler, see Thomas Fleming, *1776: Year of Illusions* (New York, 1975), 384. For Carroll, see Hoffman, *A Spirit of Dissension*, 181.

[41] Thomas Jefferson to Edmund Pendleton, August 13, 1776, Julian P. Boyd et al., eds., *The Papers of Thomas Jefferson* (Princeton, 1950-), I, 492.

more cautious about committing themselves to a government with a record of abandoning its supporters to the wrath of its enemies. In short, Princeton made a very large contribution to the winning of American independence, an achievement that the community and college needed if only to console themselves for the immense devastation they experienced in the campaign.[42]

The victories at Trenton and Princeton and the surrender of General John Burgoyne's army at Saratoga in October 1777 together gave Congress a chance to complete the Articles of Confederation. The drift toward decentralized authority became ever more explicit. Burke's states-rights clause carried easily against the opposition of James Wilson of Pennsylvania, usually considered a conservative, and Richard Henry Lee, who is normally classed as a radical.[43] When Congress finally sent off the document to the states for ratification in November 1777, the Articles provided for state sovereignty as well as state equality and gave Congress no power to tax or regulate trade. To pass, even minor measures needed the support of seven states while major issues required nine, which meant that small minorities could block motions unless attendance was very full, a problem that grew increasingly acute toward the end of the war. Congress asked the states to approve the Articles before March 10, 1778, but only Virginia met the deadline without adding amendments unacceptable to Congress. By the end of the year, Delaware and Maryland still refused, the last resisting until March 1, 1781. The holdouts were all smaller states without charter claims to western lands. Maryland remained especially adamant that it would not ratify unless Virginia agreed to surrender to the United States its alleged rights to the Northwest territories.[44]

---

[42] John Shy, "The American Revolution: The Military Conflict as a Revolutionary War," in Stephen G. Kurtz and James H. Hutson, eds., *Essays on the American Revolution* (Chapel Hill, 1973), 121-56; Alfred Hoyt Bill, *The Campaign of Princeton, 1776-1777* (Princeton, 1948); Joseph J. Casino, "Promises and Plunder: The Failure of British Counterinsurgent Policy in America, 1776-1777," John M. Murrin, ed., *War and Society in Early America from the Aztecs to the Civil War* (Philadelphia, forthcoming); John M. Murrin, "Princeton and the American Revolution," *Princeton University Library Chronicle*, xxxviii (1976-77), 1-10.

[43] See above, n. 37.

[44] Merrill Jensen et al., eds., *The Documentary History of the Ratification of the*

Several factors help to explain this gradual erosion of congressional authority. One of the most important was the constitutional revolution within the states. In 1775-1776, Congress implicitly defined its constitutional orbit by taking upon itself, not the former jurisdiction of Parliament, but the powers of the imperial crown.[45] In other words, the legislative powers of Parliament tended to devolve upon the states, while the executive powers of the crown passed to Congress, which we should probably conceptualize as more of a plural executive than a legislature. In this capacity, Congress presided over the revolutionary efforts of provincial governments, most of which at this stage were equally improvised. When a patriot provincial congress duelled for power against a neutral or loyalist assembly elected in accordance with traditional principles, Congress could tip the balance, as it did in both Pennsylvania and New Jersey on the eve of independence. Patriots were willing to let Congress decide which government was legitimate. In a truly revolutionary situation in which inherited institutions were crumbling everywhere, Congress thus provided a principle of stability to which patriots eagerly turned.

But in 1776 and 1777, most of the states drafted and adopted new constitutions. By the time Congress completed the Articles, the states had acquired a kind of legitimacy that Congress did not possess. And the disparity grew after 1777, especially once Massachusetts provided the definitive model of American constitution making in 1779-1780. Thereafter a proper constitution had to be drafted by a convention elected for that specific purpose, and the convention's efforts had to be ratified by the people. Americans had found a viable way to separate legislative power from ultimate constitutional authority. They had learned how to institutionalize their concept of the people as constituent power.[46]

Constitution (Madison, Wis., 1976-), I, 96-137; Jensen, *The Articles of Confederation*, Ch. IX-XII.

[45] Jerrilyn Greene Marston, "King and Congress: The Transfer of Political Legitimacy from the King to the Continental Congress, 1774-1776" (Ph.D. dissertation, Boston University, 1975).

[46] See generally Robert R. Palmer, *The Age of the Democratic Revolution: A Political History of Europe and America, 1760-1800*, 2 vols. (Princeton, 1959-64), I, Ch. VIII; Willi Paul Adams, *The First American Constitutions: Republican Ideology*

Congress did not fare well in this competition for legitimacy, as several observers would recognize by the 1780s. "The success of the Revolution was owing to other causes, than the Constitution of Congress," declared James Wilson with a touch of quiet understatement at the Philadelphia Convention in 1787.[47] Some days earlier he had drawn upon his six years of experience in Congress to make this point more explicit. "Among the first sentiments expressed in the first Congs. one was that Virga. is no more. That Massts. is no [more], that Pa. is no more &c. We are now one nation of brethren. We must bury all local interests & distinctions." But, he told the convention, these attitudes did not last. "No sooner were the State Govts. formed than their jealousy & ambition began to display themselves. Each endeavoured to cut a slice from the common loaf, to add to its own morsel, till at length the confederation became frittered down to the impotent condition in which it now stands." Wilson saw this process very much at work in the drafting of the Articles. "Review the progress of the articles of Confederation thro' Congress & compare the first & last draught of it," he urged.[48] A "new sett of ideas seemed to have crept in since the articles of Confederation were established," complained Oliver Ellsworth of Connecticut to the same body. "Conventions of the people, or with power derived expressly from the people, were not then thought of," he insisted. "The Legislatures were considered as competent."[49] The implication seemed obvious to George Mason of Virginia. "A National Constitution derived from such a source [i.e., resting only on the approval of the state legislatures] would be exposed to the severest criticisms."[50] The revolutionary experience itself, especially its capacity to institutionalize its deepest political aspirations, had simply left Congress behind.

Other factors weakening Congress were rather more tangible.

---

and the Making of the State Constitutions in the Revolutionary Era (Chapel Hill, 1980); Gordon S. Wood, The Creation of the American Republic, 1776-1787 (Chapel Hill, 1969).

[47] Max Farrand, ed., The Records of the Federal Convention of 1787, rev. ed. (New Haven, 1937), I, 343.

[48] Ibid., 166-67.

[49] Ibid., II, 91.

[50] Ibid., 89.

After independence, the quality of men serving in that body tended to decline. Some, such as Patrick Henry and Thomas Jefferson in Virginia, returned to the states to fight the Revolution at that level while others, such as Benjamin Franklin, John Adams and John Jay, went abroad to serve the nation as diplomats.[51] The fiction of a government firmly united in a common cause became harder to maintain by 1777, and as that year ended, roll call votes became a routine device in Congress—a revealing index of emerging factionalism.[52] Even a seemingly unmitigated benefit, the French Alliance of 1778, for example, took years before it brought the advantages expected of it. It did, of course, keep the British Army on the strategic defensive in 1778 and 1779, but it also brought a French fleet to North America and later a French army, both of which had to be supplied and fed out of rapidly dwindling resources.[53] Clearly the Revolution had become a war of attrition, and when the Continental dollar utterly collapsed in 1779 and Congress agreed to print no more money, a major crisis was at hand. Congress was more dependent on the states than ever before, and they too were reaching the limit of their resources.[54]

When the British resumed the offensive in the deep South in late 1779 and 1780, the Revolution again wavered on the edge of disintegration. In rapid succession, the Americans lost two armies, one with the surrender of Charleston on May 12, 1781, and the other with General Horatio Gates' disastrous rout at Camden on August 16.[55] Benedict Arnold almost succeeded in turning West Point over to the British.[56] Throughout 1780 and 1781, the soldiers under Washington's direct command, poorly fed and miserably

[51] For two contemporary observations on this pattern, see John Adams as quoted in Edmund Cody Burnett, *The Continental Congress* (New York, 1941), 234; and George Washington to John Parke Custis, February 28, 1781, Fitzpatrick, ed., *The Writings of George Washington*, xxi, 320.

[52] Henderson, *Party Politics*, esp. 160-64.

[53] Richard Buel, Jr., *Dear Liberty: Connecticut's Mobilization for the Revolutionary War* (Middletown, Ct., 1980), 159-60.

[54] *Ibid.*, Ch. v; E. James Ferguson, *The Power of the Purse: A History of American Public Finance, 1776-1790* (Chapel Hill, 1961), Ch. ii-iii.

[55] Russell F. Weigley, *The Partisan War: The South Carolina Campaign of 1780-1782*, South Carolina Tricentennial Booklet No. 2 (Columbia, S. C., 1970).

[56] Charles Royster, " 'The Nature of Treason': Revolutionary Virtue and American Reactions to Benedict Arnold," *William and Mary Quarterly*, 3rd ser., xxxvi (1979), 163-93.

clothed, showed an understandable but nonetheless ominous tendency to mutiny.[57] The ability of the United States to maintain an army and fight a war was put to the supreme test—and was found wanting. By 1781 there probably were more armed loyalists serving with the British than Continentals enlisted under Washington.[58] In that year the French fleet and army became absolutely indispensable to a decisive American victory.[59]

In the months before Yorktown, Congress attempted to reform the faltering central government of the United States. Military disaster brought men of distinguished reputation back into Congress, and with broad support from most state legislatures, they did sponsor a fairly energetic response to the crisis.[60] Even before Maryland finally ratified the Articles, Congress completed a series of internal reforms that transferred executive authority to separate departments of finance, foreign affairs, war, and marine. The new arrangement was undoubtedly more efficient than the committee system that Congress had been using, but the results never met expectations.[61] As the war neared its close, the army became better fed and supplied, if not paid, but it was also much smaller than the forces Washington had commanded from 1775 through 1778. Robert Morris, the first Superintendent of Finance, tried to create an orthodox fiscal system for the United States. He persuaded Pennsylvania to charter the Bank of North America and Congress to ask the states for an amendment to the Articles that would enable

[57] Charles Royster, *A Revolutionary People at War: The Continental Army and American Character, 1775-1783* (Chapel Hill, 1979), Ch. vii; Carl Van Doren, *Mutiny in January: The Story of a Crisis in the Continental Army Now for the First Time Fully Told from Many Hitherto Unknown or Neglected Sources both American and British* (New York, 1943).

[58] This statement is an educated guess based primarily upon Paul H. Smith, "The American Loyalists: Notes on Their Organization and Numerical Strength," *William and Mary Quarterly*, 3rd ser., xxv (1968), 259-77; and Charles H. Lesser, ed., *The Sinews of Independence: Monthly Strength Reports of the Continental Army* (Chicago, 1976), xxxi.

[59] Jonathan R. Dull, *Lafayette, Franklin, and the Coming of Rochambeau's Army: An Address* (Morristown, N. J. 1980), 15-24.

[60] E. Wayne Carp, "The Origins of the Nationalist Movement of 1780-1783: Congressional Administration and the Continental Army," *Pennsylvania Magazine of History and Biography*, cvii (1983), 363-92; E. Wayne Carp, *"To Starve the Army at Pleasure": Continental Army Administration and American Political Culture, 1775-1783* (Chapel Hill, 1984), esp. Ch. viii.

[61] Sanders, *Evolution of the Executive Departments, passim.*

the United States to levy an impost of 5% on all imports. With these devices, he hoped to create the kind of funded national debt that had permitted England to become a great power at the end of the seventeenth century.[62] Other delegates, fearful that the crisis of 1780-1781 was too severe to wait for the results of such measures, favored giving Congress the power to coerce states into proper cooperation. To win the war against Britain, the United States might have to make war among themselves.[63]

Of the proposed reforms, only the first—the creation of executive departments—was fully implemented. Rhode Island flatly refused to ratify the impost in late 1782, and Congress never did acquire the authority to coerce a state. The army survived, but so did the danger of serious mutiny. Even the establishment of executive departments probably had one major, unintended consequence. It completed the evolution of Congress from a surrogate for the crown to a weak substitute for Parliament, from a plural executive to a feeble legislature. Once Congress provided executive bodies distinct from itself, virtually every inclination of eighteenth-century political thought compelled contemporaries to think of it as a legislature whose will the department heads would execute. As the American answer to royal prerogative, Congress had often been impressive in its early years. As a legislature, it could never inspire awe. It could not tax, nor regulate commerce, nor in any meaningful sense *legislate* for individuals. It had no judicial arm to enforce its commands. If the survival of the United States came to depend on the efficiency and effective authority of Congress, the republic would be in grave difficulty.

Fortunately for the Revolution, the British faced equally daunting obstacles. Britain too was approaching exhaustion. When Cornwallis led his battalions into a potential cul de sac at Yorktown,

[62] E. James Ferguson, "The Nationalists of 1781-1783 and the Economic Interpretation of the Constitution," *Journal of American History*, LVI (1969-70), 241-61; E. James Ferguson, "Political Economy, Public Liberty, and the Formation of the Constitution," *William and Mary Quarterly*, 3rd ser., XL (1983), 389-412; John M. Murrin, "The Great Inversion, or, Court versus Country: A Comparison of the Revolution Settlements in England (1688-1721) and America (1776-1816)," J. G. A. Pocock, ed., *Three British Revolutions: 1641, 1688, 1776* (Princeton, 1980), 368-453.

[63] Jensen et al., eds., *Documentary History of the Ratification of the Constitution*, I, 141-45.

Washington seized the opportunity. With the swift and able co-operation of Rochambeau's army and de Grasse's fleet, Washington compelled Cornwallis to surrender his entire force on October 19, 1781.[64] When the scope of this disaster became known in London, Lord North's government finally fell in March 1782, and the new ministry accepted the need to end the war and recognize American independence. The terms of any such treaty had yet to be negotiated and would decide such important issues as title to the land between the Appalachians and the Mississippi, and whether Americans had access to the North Atlantic fisheries. But by 1782 Britain had abandoned all serious efforts to subdue North America.[65]

Nevertheless, the triumph of the United States somehow led to the further humiliation of Congress. When Rhode Island in late 1782 flatly rejected the impost amendment, public creditors and army officers grew desperate. They demanded a new impost amendment that would pay the interest on the securities of public creditors and also give the officers a large commutation payment in place of the half-pay pension for life that many of them had demanded. To win these objectives, some of the younger officers were even willing to toy with the threat of a coup d'état, and they received quiet encouragement from some of the centralizers in Congress. In a dramatic confrontation at the Continental Army encampment at Newburgh, New York in mid-March 1783, Washington faced down his angry officers and reasserted control. Fumbling at one point for his spectacles so that he could read a letter to the assembled men, he mumbled that he had grown gray in the service of his country and now found that he was going blind. The prospects for a real coup disintegrated as mature adults wept openly at this gesture. Deeper forces were also at work. After all, a coup can succeed only when armed men can grasp the levers of power. In the United States in 1783, power was so decentralized that even had the army captured the entire Congress, it would have gained little real control over the country at large. The more perceptive officers involved in the affair understood this point and probably intended no more than a bluff, but such matters do have a way of

[64] Thomas Fleming, *Beat the Last Drum: The Siege of Yorktown, 1781* (New York, 1963) is a spirited and intelligent account.
[65] Richard B. Morris, *The Peacemakers: The Great Powers and American Independence* (New York, 1965).

going farther than anyone first intends. At the very least, the principle of military subordination to the civil power seemed on the line in 1783.[66]

Congress survived this challenge from army officers only to fall victim to the rage and impatience of ordinary soldiers. With the war all but over, Congress decided to cut expenses and prevent further embarrassments by furloughing to their homes most of the soldiers still in service. For their part, the men had not been paid since sometime in 1782, and many were reluctant to accept a furlough before Congress had at least settled accounts with them, a process that Robert Morris believed would take several years. Washington soothed the troops at Newburgh by making the furlough optional, not mandatory, which meant that the garrison did gradually melt away. This order did not reach the Third Pennsylvania Regiment of the Continental Line stationed at Lancaster, Pennsylvania, most of whom were recent recruits, not combat veterans. About eighty of them decided to march on Philadelphia and demand justice, not from Congress, but from the state of Pennsylvania, which undoubtedly had access to greater resources in 1783 than the government of the United States. In Philadelphia the men of the Third linked with veterans from other units who were either part of the garrison stationed in the city or had recently returned from General Nathanael Greene's brilliantly successful campaign in the deep South. With numbers now swollen to three hundred or more and with their sergeants and two junior officers for leaders, the dissidents approached the State House around midday on Saturday, June 21. Marching in good order with bayonets fixed, they surrounded the building and presented an ultimatum to the Pennsylvania Supreme Executive Council which was then sitting on the second floor with John Dickinson acting as president. The soldiers demanded the right to choose their own officers to negotiate their grievances with the Council. They insisted on a reply within twenty minutes, or else, as Elias Boudinot recounted, "they would turn . . . an enraged Soldiery on the Council, who would do themselves

---

[66] Richard H. Kohn, "The Inside History of the Newburgh Conspiracy: America and the Coup d'Etat," *William and Mary Quarterly*, 3rd ser., xxvii (1970), 187-220.

Elias Boudinot by Charles Willson Peale
Oil on canvas. Gift of Mr. and Mrs. Landon K. Thorne
The Art Museum, Princeton University

Justice, and the Council must abide the consequences, or words to that effect."[67]

Congress, which routinely met on the first floor of the same building, had no regular session scheduled for that Saturday. The soldiers presumably were aware of this fact. But Boudinot, the President of Congress, summoned an emergency session on thirty-minutes' notice, and it gathered at about the time the soldiers arrived. Because only six states and a few other delegates were present, the meeting lacked a quorum and was not a legal sitting of the Congress of the United States. Nor did the soldiers communicate with Congress, threaten it specifically, or make any explicit demands on it. Dickinson informed Boudinot of the soldiers' manifesto and, with the backing of his Council, proceeded to negotiate with the mutineers. Boudinot, supported by virtually all the delegates present, demanded that Dickinson summon the Philadelphia militia and quash the disturbance. Dickinson, the Executive Council, and apparently most of the citizens of Philadelphia sympathized with the army's grievances, doubted that the militia would respond to a mission that might require them to fire upon veterans of American victories in the South, and therefore supported a peaceful solution. The mere promise to negotiate did work, for the soldiers returned to their barracks later that afternoon.

As Kenneth Bowling has argued, Congress was probably just as mortified by the *lack* of attention it received as by the actual mutiny. Continental soldiers subject to the direct command of Congress looked to Pennsylvania, not the United States, for redress. Pennsylvania's Supreme Executive Council worried more about the needs and demands of the army than about the dignity of Congress. A North Carolina delegate nicely expressed this sense of utter humiliation, which he feared might prove "perhaps fatal to the Union." "In this State of things what can Congress do," asked Benjamin Hawkins, "without the means of paying those Debts they Constitutionally contracted for the safety of the United States, responsible

---

[67] Kenneth R. Bowling, "New Light on the Philadelphia Mutiny of 1783: Federal-State Confrontation at the Close of the War for Independence," *Pennsylvania Magazine of History and Biography*, CI (1977), 419-50; Elias Boudinot to George Washington, June 21, 1783, Edmund Cody Burnett, ed., *Letters of Members of the Continental Congress* (Washington, D. C., 1921-36), VII, 193-94.

Nassau Hall, 1764. Copperplate engraving drawn by W. Tennent,
engraved by H. Dawkins. Princeton University Library

for every thing, and unable to do any thing, hated by the public
creditors, insulted by the Soldiery and unsupported by the citizens?"[68]

Within Congress centralizers and localists could both agree that
they had been insulted. Armed men had surrounded and threatened the building while Congress tried to meet inside, and no one
seemed much inclined to do anything to sooth its battered dignity.
Rather more surprisingly, the delegates could also agree on proper
remedies. Boudinot wrote Washington to send reliable troops to
restore order, and Congress decided that it must leave Philadelphia.
Nationalists hoped that this gesture would provide dramatic con-
firmation of the need for more power in the government of the
United States. Opponents of centralization took comfort from the

[68] Benjamin Hawkins to Alexander Martin, June 24, 1783, *ibid.*, 199; Bowling, "New Light on the Philadelphia Mutiny of 1783," *passim*.

realization that removal would put salutary distance between Congress and Robert Morris, the leading nationalist.[69]

Acting swiftly and quietly, Congress agreed on Tuesday, June 24, to remove to Princeton, where Boudinot had excellent social contacts and had already arranged a friendly reception. Two days later the delegates began to arrive in the small college town of sixty to eighty houses. During the war the British Army had twice driven Congress from Philadelphia. This time, however, Congress was fleeing the city and its own executive offices because of a rising among soldiers who did not even wish to talk with it. The departure of Congress was thus fraught with ambiguous implications. Benjamin Hawkins apparently believed that removal was a necessary step to preserve the Union. Charles Thomson worried that the Union would be in ever graver peril the longer Congress remained away. Boudinot insisted that Dickinson and Pennsylvania owed Congress a formal apology and a specific invitation to return. Dickinson thought he had handled the crisis humanely and intelligently and was in no mood to apologize. Because these issues were not easily compromised, Congress had in effect condemned itself to becoming a wanderer over the next several years as it moved from Philadelphia to Princeton to Annapolis to Trenton and finally New York.[70]

We shall not here recount the story of Congress at Princeton, which has been well told by others.[71] For four months a crossroads village became the capital of the United States, to the considerable discomfort of both the statesmen and, one presumes, most of the inhabitants. High points of the congressional stay included celebration of the Fourth of July, ratification of a commercial treaty with Sweden, the arrival of General Washington in August for a two-month visit, perhaps the most illustrious commencement exercises in the entire history of the college in September, an elaborate

[69] See Boudinot to Washington, June 21, 1783, and Boudinot's Proclamation of June 24, 1783, in Burnett, ed., *Letters of Members of the Continental Congress,* VII, 194, 195-96.

[70] See generally Lawrence Delbert Cress, "Whither Columbia? Congressional Residence and the Politics of the New Nation, 1776 to 1787," *William and Mary Quarterly,* 3rd ser., XXXII (1975), 581-600.

[71] Varnum L. Collins, *The Continental Congress at Princeton* (Princeton, 1908); Gary B. Nash, ". . . *and Distinguished Guests": The Continental Congress at Princeton, 1783* (Princeton, 1962).

reception in October for the Dutch minister to the United States, and on October 31—just four days before Congress left for Annapolis—the receipt by special express of the joyous news that the definitive peace treaty had been signed in Paris.

Amidst all the festivities, Congress could not forget its continuing difficulties. Boudinot's (and Alexander Hamilton's) duel with Dickinson would not subside. More fundamentally, Congress throughout its stay at Princeton could seldom muster a quorum of seven states, much less the nine necessary to ratify a treaty. The move to Annapolis meant still greater delays. Congress could not even produce a quorum to ratify the peace treaty guaranteeing American independence within the time limit that the treaty required. Nor could it afford even to pay a courier to take the news of its tardy action back to Europe. The French minister, the Chevalier de La Luzerne, had to use French money to pay a British ship captain to consummate this final act of American independence.[72]

As secretary, Charles Thomson had served the Congress for nine years by late 1783, longer and more continuously than anyone else. The removal from Philadelphia compelled him to communicate by letter with his beloved wife Hannah, and we are much the richer for this necessity. Always exceptionally well informed, his letters tell a fascinating story. Not only do they provide an agreeable glance into the private life of an important but rather neglected patriot. They also illuminate the immense difficulties that beset the new American republic at what should have been its moment of supreme vindication and triumph.

[72] William C. Stinchcombe, *The American Revolution and the French Alliance* (Syracuse, 1969), 210.

CONGRESS AT PRINCETON

LIST OF ABBREVIATIONS

Bio. Dir. Cong.   *Biographical Directory of the American Congress, 1774-1971*, Washington, D. C., 1971.

Burnett, *Letters*   Edmund C. Burnett, ed., *Letters of Members of the Continental Congress, 1774-1789*, 8 vols., Washington, D. C., 1921-1936.

DAB   Allen Johnson and Dumas Malone, eds., *Dictionary of American Biography*, 20 vols., New York, 1928-1936.

JCC   Worthington C. Ford et al., eds., *Journals of the Continental Congress, 1774-1789*, 34 vols., Washington, D. C., 1904-1937.

MS   Manuscript.

PCC   Papers of the Continental Congress, National Archives, Washington, D. C.

PMHB   *Pennsylvania Magazine of History and Biography.*

Princetonians   James McLachlan et al., *Princetonians: A Biographical Dictionary*, 3 vols., Princeton, 1976-.

RC   Recipient's copy of letter.

❖

Dear Hannah,   Monday June 30. 1783.

By nine o clock, the evening I left you, I arrived at Bristol, where I met the Minister[1] on his return. He informed me that a sufficient number of states had not yet met to proceed to business. He expressed a great desire that Congress would return, and was anxious that their removal should not even be known in Europe by any public act done out of Philadelphia. Next day I started a little after three and was in the boat at Trenton ferry before Six. The ride thus far was exceedingly pleasant, the morning Serene, and the air cool and refreshing. At Trenton I shaved, washed & breakfasted & waited till eight in hopes of seeing Govr. Morris.[2] Mr. R. M.[3]

RC (Princeton University Library: Charles Thomson Papers).

[1] Anne-César, Chevalier de La Luzerne (1741-91), a French diplomat who later served as ambassador to Great Britain, was France's minister to the United States from 1779 to 1784. See William E. O'Donnell, *The Chevalier de La Luzerne: French Minister to the United States, 1779-1784* (Bruges, Belgium, 1938).

[2] Gouverneur Morris (1752-1816), a New York landed aristocrat and graduate of King's College, 1768, served in Congress from 1778 to 1779 and then chose to live in Pennsylvania after the New York legislature refused to select him for another congressional term. Morris accepted an appointment as assistant superintendent of finance of the United States from Robert Morris in 1781 and held this office for four years. See Max Mintz, *Gouverneur Morris and the American Revolution* (Norman, Oklahoma, 1970).

[3] Robert Morris (1734-1806), a wealthy Philadelphia merchant who had been a highly influential member of Congress from 1775 to 1778, served as superintendent of finance of the United States from 1781 to 1784. During his tenure in office Morris sought to enhance the power of Congress and to promote American economic development by advocating the adoption of an ambitious program that among other things called for funding the national debt, granting taxing authority to Congress, creating a national bank, and transferring to Congress the responsibility for paying the debts incurred by the states as part of the war effort. Morris' program, which foreshadowed many of the policies later adopted by Alexander Hamilton, was generally unsuccessful owing to the opposition of supporters of state sovereignty, who feared that the measures he proposed would eventually make Congress more powerful than the states. It was this fear of centralization, coupled with the conviction on the part of a number of delegates that Morris corruptly took advantage of his public office to advance his private interests, that accounts for the hostility to the superintendent of finance described by Thomson in some of his subsequent letters to his wife. Thomson's willingness to defend Morris against his congressional critics is in turn a revealing index of the extent to which he had been nationalized by his years of service as secretary to Congress. See Clarence L. Ver

Hannah Harrison Thomson by Matthew Pratt
Oil on canvas. Collection of Armistead Peter, 3rd
Courtesy of the Frick Art Reference Library

had left town just before I got in to meet Mrs. M. at Bristol and as he crossed at another ferry I missed him. Govr. was gone a fishing and though I sent him a note to inform him of my arrival, I suppose he thought it too great a sacrifice to forego the pleasure of fishing. As soon as I had breakfasted I set forward and travelling easy I arrived at Princeton about eleven. I had a fine air in my face but the sun beams were excessively hot & scorching. I drove up immediately to Col. Morgan's which is just behind the college in a most elegant situation commanding an extensive and delightful prospect.[4] I have a parlour below stairs & a chamber above which though small is clean, cool and pleasant. Mrs. Morgan is easy, polite and agreeable as the colonel. The Col. has thrown aside the citizen and put on the country gentleman, and enjoys that situation in life which in my Opinion is the most delightful. He has a farm of two hundred acres of good land, and enjoys the benefit of an Agreeable society. The town is small not much larger than Newark and the chief part of the houses small & built of wood. There are a number of genteel houses around & in the neighborhood. With respect to situation, convenience & pleasure I do not know a more agreeable spot in America. As soon as I had dressed I went to the College to meet Congress.[5] I was conducted along an entry (which runs from

---

Steeg, *Robert Morris: Revolutionary Financier. With an Analysis of His Earlier Career* (Philadelphia, 1954).

[4] George Morgan (1743-1810), a Pennsylvania merchant and land speculator, served Congress as an Indian agent in the Middle Department from 1775 to 1779, when he retired to Prospect, his estate in Princeton. There, aside from a brief interval in the late 1780s when he helped to found the colony of New Madrid in Spanish Louisiana, he lived as a gentleman farmer and amateur agricultural scientist until he returned to his native state in 1796. See Max Savelle, *George Morgan: Colony Builder* (New York, 1932).

[5] This statement disproves Varnum L. Collins' hitherto plausible conjecture that Congress met at George Morgan's Prospect estate between June 30, when the delegates first officially gathered to transact business in Princeton, and July 2, when they accepted the College of New Jersey's offer to use Nassau Hall as a meeting place for Congress. As Collins pointed out, Col. Morgan offered Congress the use of Prospect on June 25 and later described one of the rooms in his home as the "Congress Room," but Thomson's testimony that on June 30 he went "to the College to meet Congress" clearly demonstrates that the delegates were already convened in Nassau Hall and thus could not have met at Prospect on the dates Collins surmised. Perhaps certain members of Congress met informally at Prospect before the 30th, but it is certain they did not transact any public business there. See Varnum L. Collins, *The Continental Congress at*

one end to the other through the middle of the college) & was led
up into the third story where a few members were assembled.
Whether it was design or accident that led me this way, I know not.
But it had the effect of raising my mortification & disgust at the
Situation of Congress to the highest degree. For as I was led along
the entry I passed by the chambers of the students, from whence
in the sultry heat of the day issued warm steams from the beds,
foul linen & dirty lodgings of the boys. I found the members extremely out of humour and dissatisfied with their situation. They
are quartered upon the inhabitants who have put themselves to
great inconveniencies to receive them into their houses & furnish
them with lodgings, but who are not in a situation to board them.
The letter I brought from the Prest. of the State[6] was not calculated
to remove their uneasiness or heal the wound they had received.
It was dry and laconic and contained nothing that invited a return.
When I left col. Morgan's I asked him whether I was to board as
well as lodge with him. He told me he should be glad of my Com-

---

Princeton (Princeton, 1908), 55-59; as well as George Morgan to Congress, June
25, 1783, and Address of the Inhabitants of Princeton to Congress, October
13, 1783, PCC, item 46, fols. 67, 123-26.

[6] John Dickinson (1732-1808), the noted Delaware and Pennsylvania lawyer,
pamphleteer, and revolutionary leader who was the author of the celebrated
Letters from a Pennsylvania Farmer and the principal moderate spokesman in
Congress from 1774 to 1776, served as president of Pennsylvania from 1782
to 1785. Thomson and Dickinson were political allies in the struggle against
British colonial policies from the time of the Stamp Act Crisis until the meeting
of the First Continental Congress in the fall of 1774, but thereafter their paths
diverged in consequence of Thomson's lack of sympathy with Dickinson's untiring efforts to reconcile the colonies and the mother country and his disappointment with Dickinson's refusal to sign the Declaration of Independence.
The letters in this volume also reveal that Thomson attributed Congress' decision to leave Philadelphia in part to Dickinson's failure to deal promptly and
effectively with the recent mutiny of elements of the Pennsylvania Line in that
city which triggered Congress' exodus. See Milton E. Flower, *John Dickinson:
Conservative Revolutionary* (Charlottesville, Va., 1983). On June 30 Congress read
three letters from Dickinson, which described the measures taken by the government of Pennsylvania to quell the mutiny and were dated June 25, 26, and
27, 1783. Thomson delivered the last of these letters to Congress. PCC, item
38, fols. 127-31, 135, 143. For a detailed account of the mutiny, see Kenneth
R. Bowling, "New Light on the Philadelphia Mutiny of 1783: Federal-State
Confrontation at the Close of the War for Independence," PMHB, CI (1977),
419-50.

pany to dine with him as oft as was convenient & particularly that day but informed me he understood the gentlemen had agreed upon a plan of dining together at a tavern and had appointed a comee. to make the necessary arrangements[7] and that the gentlemen only breakfasted at their quarters. As that was the case I told him I would not trouble him, as I knew the hours of Congress would ill suit with rural œconomy and that I would dine with the gentlemen though I was much afraid it would not answer well with my accustomed & regular mode of living.

Ellery[8] & Arnold[9] had not yet arrived, so that there were not states sufficient to proceed to business. I had passed Ellery on the road about two miles from Philada. & expected to meet him in the evening at Bristol; but he did not come up & did not reach Princetown till late on Saturday Evening. After some conversation about the news from Philada. and present situation of Affairs the Prest.[10] adjourned Congress to meet again on Monday. He then told me he expected my company to dine with him. I said I understood the gentlemen had agreed to dine together at a tavern, and as their coming to this place must have been very unexpected, I fancied Mrs. Stockden (his sister at whose house he lodged)[11] could not be

---

[7] There is no mention of this committee in *JCC*.

[8] William Ellery (1727-1820), a graduate of Harvard College, 1747, was a Rhode Island lawyer and merchant who focused his attention primarily on naval affairs during his three terms in Congress—1776-79, 1781, 1783-86. See William M. Fowler, *William Ellery: A Rhode Island Politico and Lord of the Admiralty* (Metuchen, N.J., 1973).

[9] Jonathan Arnold (1741-93), a Rhode Island physician who organized and served as a surgeon in the Revolutionary Hospital of Rhode Island during the War for Independence, was a member of Congress from 1782 to 1784. *DAB*.

[10] Elias Boudinot (1740-1821), a prosperous New Jersey lawyer and a devout Presbyterian who later in life wrote a number of works predicting that the Second Coming of Christ was imminent, was a trustee of the College of New Jersey, 1772-1821, first commissary general of prisoners for the Continental Army, 1777-78, a member of Congress, 1778, 1781-83, and president of that body, 1782-83. A former resident of Princeton whose wife, Hannah Stockton Boudinot, was a member of one of the town's most distinguished families, Boudinot played a key role in inducing Congress to move to Princeton after it left Philadelphia. See George Boyd, *Elias Boudinot: Patriot and Statesman* (Princeton, 1952).

[11] Annis Boudinot Stockton (1736-1801), the mistress of Morven and a woman whose name Thomson consistently misspelled, was the sister of President Elias Boudinot; the widow of Richard Stockton, a graduate of the College of New

[7]

prepared to receive company and I had rather be excused. He told me he did not know whether the gentlemen had fixed their plan or taken arrangements for dining together though they talked of it & must certainly adopt some such measure if they continued in this place, But that he would expect my company to dine with him that day. I then enquired what plan they had adopted, & found they had yet come to no determination. Some had received invitations to dine with the president, others from private gentlemen, & some purposed to go to a tavern. I then conversed with individuals to know what steps they meant to take. Bland's [12] dignity was so hurt that he would never return. Izard[13] could never think of returning unless the citizens of Philadelphia would make reparation for the wounded honor of Congress. Hamilton's[14] resentment was

---

Jersey, 1748, who signed the Declaration of Independence; and the mother-in-law of Dr. Benjamin Rush, a graduate of the College of New Jersey, 1760, who was also a Signer. In addition to possessing a distinguished array of relations, Mrs. Stockton was also a moderately able writer of poetry whose fervent verses in praise of George Washington won her the respect and admiration of that worthy. See L. H. Butterfield, "Morven: A Colonial Outpost of Sensibility. With Some Hitherto Unpublished Poems by Annis Boudinot Stockton," *Princeton University Library Chronicle,* vi (1944-45), 1-15; and same, "Annis and the General: Mrs. Stockton's Poetic Eulogies of George Washington," *ibid.,* vii (1945-46), 19-39. The history of Morven itself is described in Alfred Hoyt Bill, *A House Called Morven: Its Role in American History, 1701-1954* (Princeton, 1954).

[12] Theodorick Bland (1742-90), a Virginia planter and physician who received an M.D. from the University of Utrecht in 1763, rose to the rank of colonel in the Continental cavalry during the War for Independence and was a member of Congress from 1780 to 1783. *DAB.*

[13] Ralph Izard (1741-1804), a South Carolina planter who was educated in England, served for two frustrating years as U.S. Commissioner to Tuscany before he was recalled by Congress in 1779 and was then a member of that body from 1782 to 1783. See Anne Izard Deas, *Correspondence of Mr. Ralph Izard of South Carolina, from the Year 1774 to 1804; with a Short Memoir* (New York, 1844).

[14] Alexander Hamilton (1757-1804), whose failure to gain admission to the College of New Jersey or to graduate from King's College did not hamper his meteoric career as a Continental Army officer, defender of the Constitution, first secretary of the treasury, and Federalist party leader, was a member of Congress from 1782 to 1783. Hamilton incurred Thomson's resentment by playing a leading role in securing Congress' removal from Philadelphia. For it was Hamilton who on June 24, 1783 drafted the crucial committee report that criticized the government of Pennsylvania for responding ineffectively to the mutiny of the Pennsylvania Line and advised President Boudinot to sum-

wholly bent against the president of the state and nothing but his ruin could satisfy him. I wished them to consult their reason and not their passions, to consider the interest of the Union and not private resentments. That a good use might be made of the late occurrence, if improved solely to the purpose of impressing the states with the necessity of taking speedy and effectual measures to comply with the obligations & perform the promises which Congress had made on their behalf. That the honor of Congress was safe if they returned speedily to their former place of residence and did not mix private passion with public measures. That the object which some seemed to have in view would I feared not answer their purpose. That an attempt to ruin the Prest. & criminate the council[15] might foment the divisions & party animosity which unhappily too much prevailed in the state but would be far from strengthening the Union & supporting the fœderal government. That by directing their resentment against the Pres. & council, or attempting to set the citizens against them, they might raise up friends & rather strengthen than ruin them. They could not be ignorant that there were many in Philada. who were unfriendly to our cause, who though they did not love the presidt. hated Congress & would espouse his cause against them or their cause against him not from a regard for one more than the other but from private resentments & with a view to embarrass public measures & that such a crop of dissensions might be sown in the state as might in the end involve it in the dispute or at least incapacitate it from pursuing those measures that were essential for the public safety. That in my Opinion the fate of America hung by a slender thread & it behoved Congress to act with caution. That I never had seen a period in which there was a greater necessity for the exercise of prudence & a temperate Conduct, & I was glad considering the temper of the members that they had not yet been able to proceed

---

mon Congress to meet at Trenton or Princeton. Boudinot promptly approved the report and on the same day issued a proclamation ordering the delegates to meet at Princeton in two days. See Harold C. Syrett et al., eds. *The Papers of Alexander Hamilton*, 26 vols. (New York, 1961-79), III, 403-7. A facsimile reproduction of Boudinot's proclamation appears in Collins, *The Continental Congress at Princeton*, opposite p. 28.

[15] That is, John Dickinson and the Pennsylvania Council.

to business. I told Hamilton freely that I entirely disapproved his plan, that I saw clearly it would give pain to the true friends of America and pleasure to its enemies: that the step Congress had yet taken required no justification of themselves or crimination of others. It was sufficient that they thought themselves in danger & removed out of the way of it & then returned to their duty and business when it was removed, and only pursued wise measures to prevent the like in future. And I wished him to reflect how far he might hazard the private characters of the present members who had but lately come to Congress, & who, it might be said, had by their rash, unwise & intemperate conduct dashed in pieces & over-turned a fabric begun by their wiser predecessors & raised to such a height by the blood of so many thousands. I found myself at times warm, however I determined to unburthen my mind.

I cannot forbear reprobating the conduct of our friend in Market Street,[16] and much I fear that his cursed pride will undo his country. He has his virtues but they are suited to other times. Could he have submitted to the least soothing language I am persuaded he would have found or at least the situation of affairs here would very soon have created a conciliating disposition in Congress. And affairs might have been restored to their formal channel. But his passions are too ungovernable and his pride too great to acknowledge an error, till I fear it will be too late.

After a good deal of Conversation with individuals & sometimes with several together, and no determination yet come to, where to dine, the presidents servant came to inform me that dinner was ready & the president waited for me. I therefore went and dined with him. There were three or four members who dined there. After dinner I had an Opportunity of conversing with the president and found he was desirous of returning. He said freely that this place would not do. The people had exerted themselves & put themselves to inconveniences to accommodate the members but it was a burden which they could not bear long. That there was no place where the Minister could be accommodated. In short it would not do. And that Congress must either go back to Philada. or

---

[16] John Dickinson, whose official residence as president of Pennsylvania was located on Market Street in Philadelphia.

John Dickinson by Charles Willson Peale
Oil on canvas
Courtesy of Independence National Historical Park Collection

remove to some other place. But that the members were not yet in temper, that they must have time to cool.

Yesterday we had news that Major genl. Howe is advancing with about Eleven hundred troops.[17] They will be in this town to day. Ellery and Arnold arrived late on Saturday evening so that to day they may proceed to business. In my next I shall be able to give you some account of their disposition. I have written with more freedom because Mr. Bond[18] carries this & will deliver it.

Peter behaves well, his horses are just under my Eye in Mr. Morgans stables & he lodges & diets with the family. My carriage is also safe under cover. I hope you and the family are well and

[17] Gen. Robert Howe (1732-86), the former commander of the Southern Military Department who had been instrumental in suppressing earlier mutinies among discontented Continental troops, was dispatched by Washington with 1,500 men to quell the mutiny of the Pennsylvania Line in Philadelphia. Congress further ordered Howe on July 2 to court martial the principal mutineers and conduct an investigation of the mutiny itself. Howe spent the rest of the summer of 1783 carrying out this mission in Philadelphia, and later in the year Congress pardoned all those who had been convicted by court martial and sentenced to punishment for taking part in the mutiny. See *JCC*, xxiv, 426-27, xxv, 564-66; and the reports Howe submitted to Congress between July 5 and September 2, 1783 in PCC, item 38, fols. 85-122.

Thomson initially cooperated with Howe's investigation and then had a change of heart. At first he advised Howe to consult Francis Bailey, a Philadelphia printer, for evidence pertaining to Capt. James Christie's involvement in the mutiny, but when Howe later wrote to ask for further assistance in identifying witnesses who might testify against Christie, Thomson returned the following reply:

"I have had the honor of receiving yr. letter of the 4 by genl. Lincoln. As the war is now terminated by a glorious peace and the late disturbance among the troops effectually quelled & as the circumstance alluded to has not an immediate relation to the charges on which Mr. Christie is to be tried, I do not, on mature reflection, think it necessary that even Mr. Bailey should be called on. If Mr. C. is found innocent I should be sorry that even a shade was cast on the character of a man who has hazarded his life in our cause. And even if he is found guilty I do not wish the crime to be aggravated by a single circumstance foreign to the matter."

In light of this letter, perhaps it was not entirely coincidental that Capt. Christie, who had in fact been deeply involved in the mutiny, was acquitted of all charges at his court martial. See Howe to Thomson, August 4, 1783, and Thomson to Howe, August 7, 1783, Charles Thomson Papers, Vol. i, Library of Congress; and Bowling, "New Light on the Philadelphia Mutiny of 1783," 436-37, 442-44.

[18] George Bond was deputy secretary of Congress, having been appointed to that position on November 16, 1779. *JCC*, xv, 1277.

that Page is a good boy.[19] I am afraid you will have some trouble with the cow. I think if she was kept in the lot and supplied with hay from Mr. Miller's & well fed twice a day with bran & well watered at least three times a day, it would save a great deal of trouble & would Answer better than suffering her to run out.

Take care of your health. Remember me to Robert, Amelia,[20] Jonathan[21] & Peter[22] & all enquiring friends. I shall desire Mr. Bond while he is in town to call for and forward your letters & to have mine delivered to you.

I am with sincere Affection, your loving husband

Cha Thomson

[19] Peter and Page were either servants or slaves of the Thomson family. See Robert McClenachan to Thomson, December 22, 1783, January 3 and 11, 1784, Charles Thomson Papers, Vol. I, Library of Congress.

[20] Robert McClenachan was married to Hannah Thomson's niece, Amelia Sophie Harrison McClenachan.

[21] Jonathan Mifflin, Jr., who briefly served as a purchasing agent for the Continental Board of War during the War for Independence, acted as Thomson's business representative in Philadelphia after Congress left Princeton and moved to Annapolis. See, for example, Mifflin's letters to Thomson of December 20, 23, and 30, 1783 in Charles Thomson Papers, Vol. I, Library of Congress.

[22] Peter Zachary Lloyd was clerk of the Pennsylvania Assembly.

Dear Hannah,   Thursday July 3. 1783.

You will judge of the situation of my mind when I tell you that it seems at least a month since I left you. Every day and every hour adds to my chagrin and vexation. How can it be otherwise, while I see folly, weakness and passion marking the characters of those who ought to be distinguished by their wisdom and prudence.

It is impossible to stay & do business here and yet from the disposition that prevails there is at present but little probability of a speedy return to Philadelphia. A public & continental use might have been made of the late occurrence; but passion has gained such ascendancy that that object seems quite lost. The 4 of July is to be celebrated here, the quality of Princeton are invited, and lamps it is said are to be hung up on Mrs. Stockden's cherry trees. I enclose you my Invitation card, by which you see I am loaded with *honorables*.[1] And no wonder. I have the honor of breakfasting at my lodging, of eating stinking fish & heavy half baked bread & drinking if I please abominable wine at a dirty tavern. On monday indeed I got some pretty good porter, but on tuesday the stock was exhausted, and yesterday I had the honor of drinking water to wash down some ill cooked victuals. But we are honorable gentlemen and we are out of Philada.

I wait impatiently for a letter from you to inform me how you are. My love to all friends. I am with sincere affection, your loving husband

Cha Thomson

RC (Princeton University Library: Charles Thomson Papers). Addressed: "Mrs. Thomson   Corner of Spruce and 4 Streets   Philadelphia."

[1] Although Mrs. Thomson wrote "see within" in the margin next to this sentence, the enclosed "Invitation card" has not been found. The invitation was undoubtedly to the 4th of July dinner hosted by President Boudinot at Morven, for which see note 1 of the next letter.

Annis Boudinot Stockton. Anonymous oil on canvas
Gift of Mr. and Mrs. Landon K. Thorne
The Art Museum, Princeton University

---❖---

Dear Hannah, Friday July 4 1783

Yesterday I received your letter of the 2. It was a cordial to my Spirits which have been in a constant agitation since I left you. I had almost determined to set out yesterday afternoon & celebrate the Anniversary of Independence with you in Philadelphia, and should certainly have done it, but that one of my horses was gutted in coming up, & I was afraid of hurting him. The conveyance by the stage is so inconvenient & disagreeable that I am quite discouraged from attempting it.[1]

You will readily judge what probability there is of finding accommodations in Princeton, when I inform you that it is a small scattered village, consisting of about 50 houses most of them low wooden buildings, several of them tumbling to pieces & some new & unfinished. There are five or six tolerable good brick houses or with brick fronts two stories high & there are several good farm houses around. Mrs. Stockden's is a little way out of town. The house is large for a country house, it has four rooms on a floor commodious but not grand. There have been gardens & walks but

RC (Princeton University Library: Charles Thomson Papers). Addressed: "Mrs. Thomson   Corner of Spruce & 4 Streets   Philadelphia."

[1] Ashbel Green (1762-1848), a graduate of the College of New Jersey, 1783, who served as president of the institution from 1812 to 1822, described how the 4th of July was celebrated in Princeton in 1783 in an autobiographical account written many years after the event:

"Not long after their [Congress'] meeting at Princeton, the national jubilee, the 4th of July, was to be celebrated; and then occurred the first instance of the Whig and Cliosophic societies appointing each an orator, to represent them as speaker before a public audience. I had the honour to be the Whig representative, and my Cliosophic competitor was a classmate, by the name of Gilbert T. Snowden. It was considered as a point of some importance which orator should speak first. This was decided by lot, and the lot was in my favour. The subject of my oration was, 'The superiority of a republican government over any other form.' Among my old papers, I not long since found a part of my speech on the occasion here referred to. Congress made a part of our audience, and the orators of the day were invited by the president of congress to dine with him and his other invited guests, at his quarters, which were with his sister, then a widow, at her seat at Morven."

See Ashbel Green, *The Life of Ashbel Green, V.D.M.* (New York, 1849), 142-43; and *Princetonians*, III, 404-20.

they are all a waste & only the traces of them left. Here the president keeps his court. A little farther on & nearly Opposite, lives Thomas Laurens,[2] where Hamilton lodges. Laurens has a good farm of about 300 acres. But the house is in a bad situation. Still farther from the village on the way to Philada. is the farm now occupied by Mr. Clymer.[3] It joins Mrs. Stockdens plantation. The house is well situated. It is more than a mile out of town. Here Mr. Fitzsimmons[4] is quartered. These are the only places I have visited. Quarters are taken for the Maryland delegates about a mile distant on the road to Brunswick. The rest are scattered up and down in the village. Bland is got into a tolerable house opposite to the College. He says he has ordered up all his furniture, that part of it is come and that he expects all his *Baggage* up this week. Whether Mrs. B. is included I know not, but the Minister thinks she will not like to leave Philada. I have some reason to think he was heartily frightened, and therefore affects greater concern for the wounded dignity of Congress. Besides he has but a little time to stay. His delegation ends in October & he cannot be continued longer. He can therefore the readier submit to inconvenience for a short time to gratify his resentment for the fright he was put in. The good of the public & continental considerations seem as yet to have little

[2] Thomas Lawrence, the son of a former mayor of Philadelphia by the same name, had purchased a 300-acre farm in Princeton in 1782. See Address of the Inhabitants of Princeton to Congress, October 13, 1783, PCC, item 46, fols. 123-26.

[3] George Clymer (1739-1813), a Pennsylvania merchant who served two terms in Congress—1776-77 and 1780-82—briefly retired to Princeton after his second term as a delegate before moving back to Pennsylvania to resume his public career as a state legislator and member of the U.S. House of Representatives. *DAB.* When Clymer was preparing to return to Pennsylvania he wrote a letter to Thomson in which he offered to rent Thomson's Philadelphia home and facetiously noted that "In the article of rent you will be guided in your demand by the best information, 'tho I am far from being indifferent as to the quantum for I would have it observed that as Princeton is neither Peru nor Mexico a return from thence is no presumption of wealth." Thomson, who received the letter when he was with Congress at Annapolis, decided not to rent his house to Clymer. See Clymer to Thomson, March 2, 1784, and Thomson to Clymer, April 3, 1784, Charles Thomson Papers, Vol. II, Library of Congress.

[4] Thomas FitzSimons (1741-1811), an Irish immigrant who became a successful merchant in Pennsylvania, was a member of Congress from 1782 to 1783. *DAB.*

influence & to be wholly lost in private passion. I hope they will revive, and that as passion subsides reason will reassume its place. At present all business is at a stand. There are only seven states represented And nothing of importance can be done without nine.[5]

Messages are gone to the states unrepresented urging them to send forward their delegates.[6]

I am glad to hear you are well & that Amelia is getting better. You do not say a word of P. Lloyd. Has he not visited you? Peter behaves well & is very attentive to his horses. You may tell Page I am pleased to hear he is a good boy but should have been still better pleased if he had fanned away the flies that were so troublesome to you.

When Mr. Bond comes up I will leave him to officiate for me and take a trip to Philadelphia. I long to see you being with sincere affection, your loving husband

Cha Thomson

P.S. I enclose the Freemans Journal[7] which contains several pieces that were agreeable to the members & operated as an Antidote to the poison of Oswald's paper.[8] As it will [be] some amusement to read the papers, I enclose three orders to the printers.

---

[5] Congress had briefly considered authorizing Thomson to determine whether certain proposals before it required the votes of seven or nine states to pass. The delegates decided not to entrust Thomson with this authority, however, because they feared "it wd. make the Secry. the Sovereign in many cases." See James Madison's Notes on Debates in Congress, February 28, 1783, in William T. Hutchinson et al., eds., *The Papers of James Madison*, 14 vols. (Chicago, Ill., and Charlottesville, Va., 1962-), VI, 301.

[6] President Boudinot wrote a circular letter on July 2, 1783 to the chief executive officers of New Hampshire, Connecticut, New York, Maryland, and Georgia, requesting them to send delegations to Congress. PCC, item 16, fol. 205.

[7] *The Freeman's Journal: or, The North American Intelligencer* was printed in Philadelphia by Francis Bailey.

[8] Eleazer Oswald and Daniel Humphreys of Philadelphia printed *The Independent Gazeteer; or, The Chronicle of Freedom.*

❖

Dear Hannah,   Sunday July 6. 1783

I can hardly persuade myself that this is only the tenth day since I left you. To me it appears more than a month. I have nothing to employ my mind but scenes and reflexions which occasion chagrin & mortification. When I look back on the occurrences & transactions of a fortnight past I see few marks of wisdom, when I look forward I see a dark cloud and gloomy prospects for America. I confess I have great apprehensions for the union of the states, & begin to fear that America will experience internal convulsions, and that the fabrick of her liberty will be stained with the blood of her sons. Those jarring principles which were kept down by common danger begin to operate, And pride & passion seem to occupy the seat of reason. Who could imagine that after ten days reflexion, the only effect produced by the late mutinous attempt & removal of C. has been the returning complimentary answers to the addresses of the inhabitants of Trenton and Princeton—Addresses evidently dictated by self interest, and with a view to engage Congress to fix its residence among them & thereby promote their private emolument & not the public good?[1] The first & great object which presented itself to my mind & the great use which might have been made of the late occurrence, was the pointing out to the states the dangerous effects produced by their not complying with the past recommendations & requisitions of C. and urging the necessity of speedy & effectual measures to fulfil the obligations entered into & the promises made by Congress on their behalf, and the danger that might & certainly would result from a farther delay. This I urged with all the force I was master of & was promised that it should be done. But the very man, who promised to move

RC (Princeton University Library: Charles Thomson Papers). Addressed: "Mrs. Thomson   Corner of Spruce and fourth Streets   Philadelphia."

[1] The addresses of the inhabitants of Trenton and Princeton to Congress, the first dated June 24 and the second June 26, 1783, both pledged support for Congress and invited the delegates to use their town as a meeting place. PCC, item 46, fols. 75-87. President Boudinot transmitted Congress' resolutions of thanks for these addresses in letters written to representatives of the two towns on July 3 and 4, 1783. PCC, item 16, fols. 206-8; and JCC, XXIV, 423-24.

for the appointment of a comee. for the purpose suffered two or three days to pass without ever mentioning it & then suddenly left Congress & returned to Philada. Others have followed his example. And here the representative sovereignty of America is left without a sufficient number of states to do any one act, and the members that remain have only to stalk along the streets of this paultry village, a spectacle of contempt & derision to disaffected passengers. It is a question with me whether we shall make a Congress this week. I was told last evening there is no expectation of one before Wednesday. Upon this I proposed to the president to return to Philada. in order to visit my family, but he objected. I shall therefore stay till Mr. Bond comes up, by which time my horses will be fit [to] travel & shall then go down: so that I think you may expect to see me next Saturday. We have had a great deal of rain these two days past. I hope you & your family are well and that Dick amuses you with his songs. The Superintendant has returned & reassumed his business in Philada.[2] The paymaster genl. has also got liberty to carry back his papers and the Assist. Secy. at war proposes to apply for leave to do the same as soon [as] seven States are assembled.[3] So that I think Congress being without its officers will soon find it improper to continue here.

I am with sincere affection, your loving husband

Cha Thomson

[2] President Boudinot expressed Congress' agreement with Robert Morris' wish to return to the superintendent of finance's offices in Philadelphia in a letter written to Morris on June 30, 1783. PCC, item 16, fols. 221-22.

[3] Congress gave Paymaster General John Pierce permission to return to Philadelphia on July 4, 1783, but Assistant Secretary of War William Jackson must have elected to remain in Princeton because most of his official correspondence during the summer and fall of 1783 bears a Princeton dateline. JCC, XXIV, 427n; and PCC, item 149, vol. III, *passim.*

My dear Hannah   July 8. 1783.

I received your welcome and very agreeable letters of the 3, 4 & 5 and that dated Sunday morning. They were all delivered to me together. I am sincerely sorry for your loss. I had flattered myself that the little charmer would have amused & diverted you in my absence with his songs. But this as well as a thousand other instances serves to shew how vain the hope "to seek for happiness beneath the skies." Besides you see how deep the love of liberty is inrooted in the breast even of animals. All your care, attention & caresses could not detain the little lovely prisoner when the prison gate was opened. Poor Dick little doest thou know what dangers await thee. Thou hast now no kind mistress to provide thy repasts and to guard thee from the ravenous hawk or the murderous gun. However since liberty is thy choice may thou find a faithful mate to solace thy cares. May thou be happy as well as free.

I think it is almost time to dismiss Mr. Du S.[1] I encouraged his visits because he served as an instrument to shew the temper of the tories & to point out how their spirits rose or fell. He was my *tory meter*. But as it is now of little importance to know how they are affected, the instrument is become useless & I care not how soon it is thrown aside. I long to see you. As I am uncertain about the conveyance I dare not express my sentiments freely. I hope to be with you Sometime this week. I enclose two letters, which you will send to Mr. White[2] & request the favour of him to forward

RC (Princeton University Library: Charles Thomson Papers). Addressed: "Mrs. Thomson."

[1] This is evidently a reference to Pierre Eugène Du Simitière (ca. 1736-84), a Swiss-born portrait painter, antiquarian, and naturalist who lived in Philadelphia for the last eighteen years of his life and strove to remain neutral during the War for Independence. See Hans Huth, "Pierre Eugène Du Simitière and the Beginnings of the American Historical Museum," PMHB, LXIX (1945), 315-25. Du Simitière painted a portrait of Thomson that appeared in Du Simitière's *Portraits of the Generals, Ministers, Magistrates, Members of Congress and Others, Who Have Rendered Themselves Illustrious in the Revolution of the United States of North America* (London, 1783), plate 5. The portrait is reproduced in Donald H. Creswell, comp., *The American Revolution in Drawings and Prints* (Washington, D.C., 1975), 62.

[2] William White, D.D. (1748-1836), a graduate of the College of Philadelphia,

that to Mr. Duffield[3] as soon as possible. My love to Jonathan, Robert and Amelia. Take care of your health & rest assured of the unfeigned affection of, my dear Hannah, your loving husband

Cha Thomson

❖

Dear Hannah   Tuesday July 22. 1783

I wait with impatience to hear how and when you got home. Tho the morning you set out was lowering & unpromising, yet the day turned out favourable. I hope you found the family well and that Dick received you with a song.

The address is not yet arrived.[1] What can be the meaning of this delay?[2] Are any tricks a playing? If it does not come this day I shall begin to suspect. Mr. Peters[3] arrived last evening but can give no account of it. He was not in town but spent Sunday at his farm.

I drank tea last evening at Mrs. Livingston's.[4] She expressed a good deal of uneasiness at not having waited on you.

Be pleased to forward the enclosed as soon as possible & let me hear from you by every opportunity.

1765, and brother-in-law of Robert Morris, was rector of Christ Church in Philadelphia before becoming Pennsylvania's first Episcopal bishop in 1787. *DAB.*

[3] George Duffield (1732-90), a graduate of the College of New Jersey, 1752, was pastor of the Third Presbyterian Church in Philadelphia. *Princetonians*, I, 51-53.

RC (Princeton University Library: Charles Thomson Papers). Addressed: "Mrs. Thomson   at the Corner of Spruce & 4 Street   Philadelphia."

[1] See Thomson to Hannah Thomson, July 24, 1783, note 1.

[2] At this point Thomson first wrote and then deleted: "If it does not come this day I shall begin to suspect some foul play."

[3] Richard Peters (1744-1828), a Pennsylvania lawyer and graduate of the College of Philadelphia, 1761, served on the Continental Board of War from 1776 to 1781 and as a delegate to Congress from 1782 to 1783. *DAB.*

[4] Susannah French Livingston was the wife of William Livingston, governor of New Jersey from 1776 to 1790.

Dear Hannah   Tuesday July 22. 1783

I wait with impatience to hear how
and when you got home. Tho the morning ——
was lowering & unpromising, yet the day turned ——
favourable. I hope you found the family well and
that Dick received you with a song.

The address is not yet arrived. What can be
the meaning of this delay? ~~————————————~~
~~————————————————————~~. Are
any tricks a playing? If it does not come this day
I shall begin to suspect. Mr Peters arrived last evening
But can give no account of it. He was not in town
but spent Sunday at his farm.

I drank tea last evening at Mrs Swingston's
She expressed a good deal of uneasiness at not having
waited on you.

Be pleased to forward the enclosed as
soon as possible & let me hear from you by every
opportunity. I am with sincere affection

Your loving husband
Cha Thomson

P.S. 12 o clock
this moment Mr Izard has rec'd a
letter from Jas Rivington dated 21 informing
that the mercury packet was just arrived at New york
& has brought the definitive & that the day appointed in
England for the evacuation of New York was the 21 July.
If you give a copy of this don't give Mr Izard's name but say a letter is
just rec'd

Letter of Charles Thomson to his wife, Hannah, July 22, 1783
Gift of the Friends of the Princeton University Library

I am with sincere affection, your loving husband

Cha Thomson

P.S. 12 o clock. This moment Mr. Izard has recd. a letter from Jas. Rivington[5] dated 21 informing that the Mercury packet was just arrived at Newyork & has brought the definitive[6] & that the day appointed in England for the evacuation of New York was the 21 July. If you give a copy of this dont give Mr. Izard's name but say a letter is just recd. &c.

---

[5] James Rivington (1724-1802), an English-born bookseller and printer, was the staunchly Loyalist publisher of the *Royal Gazette* of New York throughout the greater part of the War for Independence. As the tide of battle turned against the British, however, Rivington secretly changed sides and at some point in 1781 began to act as a spy for General Washington, taking advantage of his position as royal printer of New York to transmit sometimes vital intelligence about British military and naval operations to the Continental commander-in-chief. See Catherine Snell Crary, "The Tory and the Spy: The Double Life of James Rivington," *William and Mary Quarterly*, 3d ser., xvi (1959), 61-72. Rivington also established a clandestine relationship with Thomson, but unfortunately the only known evidence pertaining to it consists of accounts Thomson gave late in life to Mrs. Deborah Logan, a family friend, and John F. Watson, a Philadelphia antiquarian. According to Mrs. Logan:
"I have also heard him [Thomson] expressly state that Rivington, the king's printer at New York, had an understanding with Congress, and corresponded in a secret and artful manner with him, furnishing him frequently with hints that developed the latent designs of the enemy. At one time he warned him of a design to administer poison to General Washington, and mentioned the course that would be pursued, which certain circumstances seemed to corroborate. The General had at that time in his family a woman of great integrity, who managed the affairs of his household. He was sick, and to her was committed the precious trust of preparing everything he was to take, herself; which she did so, and tasted a little of all his food previous to its being served up to him. The design was after a while abandoned. This woman in the decline of life had a small pension allowed her by Congress: her name was Thompson."
See Deborah Logan to Alexander Garden, "26th Ninth Mo. 1822," in *Collections of the Historical Society of Pennsylvania*, i (1853), 120. Watson received essentially the same account of Thomson's dealings with Rivington. *Ibid.*, 91-92.
[6] The news of the arrival of the definitive peace treaty between the United States and Great Britain was premature. American and British negotiators did not sign the definitive Treaty of Paris until September 3, 1783, news of the treaty did not reach Princeton until the end of October, and Congress did not ratify it until January 14, 1784. The negotiators had signed a provisional treaty of peace on November 30, 1782, whose terms were virtually identical to those of the final treaty, and Congress had ratified it on April 15, 1783. See Hunter Miller, ed., *Treaties and Other International Acts of the United States of America*, 8 vols. (Washington, D.C., 1931-48), ii, 96-107, 151-57.

Dear Hannah   Wednesday July 23. 1783

Yesterday I sent you a letter by W. Bell which he promised to deliver last Evening. I hope you have received it & that you forwarded the enclosed. I want very much to know the reason of this unaccountable delay of the address which is not yet arrived. Cong. are in an awkward situation. They cannot here proceed to business. A sufficient number of states cannot be got together to do business. A great majority in my Opinion wish to return. But unfortunately in the heat of passion they resolved that they would not or could not consistently with their dignity return until they received an invitation & assurance of protection.[1] This has embarrassed them. It was contrary to my judgment & opinion. I wished them to pursue their own measures without depending on the sentiments of others & to stay here or return back according as circumstances and the public interest pointed out. Nay I was decidedly of opinion that, as they had removed from their usual place of residence in consequence of a mutiny of continental troops and not of any insult from the citizens, they ought to return as soon as the danger was over or they were in condition to quell the mutiny; & not to take the least public notice of the conduct of council until good order was again restored. It then might be necessary & proper to remind the Council of the impropriety of their conduct, of the insults & dangers to which their want of spirit & exertion had exposed the fœderal government and of their duty to protect and defend it. At the same time they might have called on every state in the Union in the most pressing terms to comply with the requisitions of Congress & pointed out the mischiefs & dangers which had arisen & must ensue from their non compliance. This in my opinion was the true line of dignity & propriety and had they pursued it they would now, instead of the awkward situation in which they are, be standing on high ground dictating to the states, reminding them of their duty and pointing out the way to happiness & safety. Their

RC (Princeton University Library: Charles Thomson Papers). Addressed: "Mrs. Thomson   at the Corner of Spruce & 4 Streets   Philadelphia."

[1] This resolve, which was drafted by Ralph Izard and approved by Congress on July 2, 1783, is in *JCC*, XXIV, 424-25.

conduct would have commanded respect both at home and abroad and a certain person & his council[2] upon recollection would have been covered with shame & confusion for the part they acted & I am persuaded the citizens would have found it necessary to vindicate themselves[3] by such explanations, addresses or declarations as would have been satisfactory to Congress, however they might have reflected dishonor on the Ex. Council. This was the opinion I gave on my first coming here, & which I am still persuaded was right. But through this whole affair I have been particularly unfortunate. For not one single piece of advice or sentiment suggested by me either to a certain person or to the members of C. have been attended to or followed, and you know I was not wanting in the former. I shall therefore submit and leave the event to Providence which has hitherto so remarkably interposed in Our favour.

I had the satisfaction of hearing from Mr. Duane[4] that you had got as far as Neshaminy in good time & without any accident & that you set out from thence early in the afternoon for Philada. where I hope you arrived safe. Please to make my compliments to Mrs. Morgan & tell her all her family are well and that Miss Nancy does the honors of the table with a grace, which does great credit to herself and to the instructions she must have received from her Mamma. Miss Molly is chearful as a bird and George finds a new play for every day. Master John as usual attends his book & horses. And the Colonel is as attentive as ever to his farm. In short you may tell her that they are all as happy as they can be without her company. And let me wisper to you that all the charms of Princeton cannot compensate for the want of the company of my dearest Hannah.

I am with much affection, your loving husband

Cha Thomson

[2] That is, John Dickinson and the Pennsylvania Council.

[3] Thomson first wrote "to vindicate their wounded honor" and then altered it to read as above.

[4] James Duane (1733-97), a New York lawyer and land speculator, served in Congress almost continuously from 1774 to 1783, which made him one of the most experienced members of that body. See Edward P. Alexander, *A Revolutionary Conservative: James Duane of New York* (New York, 1938).

Dear Hannah   Thursday July 24 1783

Yesterday I received your welcome note and letter with the basket, and distributed your presents as directed.

The address is at last arrived.[1] It came yesterday under cover to the delegates while Congress were sitting, for you must know they made a house yesterday. It was immediately delivered to the president, read and committed to a committee of five members. Committees generally consist of three, but when the subject is deemed to be of great importance, it is then committed to five. So that hitherto the address is treated with great respect. The report of the committee will bring the subject before the house & it will then

RC (Princeton University Library: Charles Thomson Papers). Addressed: "Mrs. Thomson   at the Corner of Spruce & 4 Streets   Philadelphia." Endorsed by Charles Thomson: "You will please to send the letters enclosed with this to Mr. Fitzsimmons as soon as you can."

[1] The address of the inhabitants of Philadelphia to Congress was an effort to undo the damage caused by the mutiny of the Pennsylvania Line and induce Congress to return to that city. This undated document, which was drafted by the noted revolutionary propagandist Thomas Paine and signed by 873 people, recounted Philadelphia's services to the Continental cause during the American Revolution and urged the delegates to keep the city in mind when they considered a permanent seat for Congress, pointing out that "the situation of Philadelphia is convenient for transacting therein the concerns of the Nation, that Congress may repose the utmost confidence in its inhabitants, not only to prevent any Circumstances which may have a tendency to disturb their necessary deliberations, but to aid in all measures to support the National honor and dignity." PCC, item 43, fols. 312-31. During a recent visit to Philadelphia Thomson had made an unsuccessful effort to strengthen this appeal even further by associating the government of Pennsylvania with it. "I called at your house but had not the pleasure of finding you at home," he had then written to President John Dickinson. "The design of my calling was to suggest a sentiment for your consideration. You know that the citizens of Philadelphia are signing an address to Congress. I am told it has been shewn to you—and that you do not disapprove it. Might it not be proper for council to forward the address & accompany it with something conciliatory from themselves. If you approve this and Council will adopt the measure, I think ways & means may be devised to induce the Citizens to forward their address through that channel." See Charles Thomson to John Dickinson, July 11, 1783, Charles Thomson Papers, Vol. I, Library of Congress. Dickinson's failure to follow Thomson's suggestion about lending the Pennsylvania Executive Council's official sanction to the Philadelphia address was undoubtedly one of the reasons why Congress eventually made a noncommittal response to it.

be determined whether Congress shall stay here or return to Philada.[2] Mr. Morgan was indisposed yesterday, but to day he thinks himself pretty well. I am glad you got home before this hot weather. I think last evening exceeded any I ever felt. I hope you will take care of your health. My love to all friends. I am, with sincere affection, your loving husband

Cha Thomson

❖

Dear Hannah,   Friday July 25. 1783

I informed you in my last that the Address arrived on Wednesday and was referred to a committee. Yesterday only six states attended so that nothing could be done and it is a doubt with me whether there will be states enough to day to form a Congress for business. Mrs. Morgan and her brother came up in the stage yesterday. The weather was so extremely hot that the passengers suffered greatly. Some of the horses dropped down & died & the rest came in excessively jaded. It was the same with the stages from Elizabeth town, which were obliged to leave the passengers on the road, some of whom walked into this town through the broiling sun & fresh horses were sent to bring in others. I think I never felt such a night and day as yesterday and the night before. Last Evening a fine breeze sprung up which continues this morning and is very re- freshing. I hope you take care of your health.

I forgot to tell you that there are 873 names to the address sent up. That with Reed's emendations is not sent up.[1] What an ill fated

---

[2] See Thomson to Hannah Thomson, July 29, 1783, note 3.

RC (Princeton University Library: Charles Thomson Papers). Addressed: "Mrs. Thomson."

[1] Joseph Reed (1741-85), a Pennsylvania lawyer and political leader who graduated from the College of New Jersey in 1757 and studied law at the Middle Temple in London, was nearing the end of a varied public career in

wretch he is! He might have made some advantage of this business and if he could not have raised himself he might have gratified his infernal malice by depressing his enemy had he joined heartily in the address. But his fondness of being at the head of a party will leave him just as this affair found him: hated, despised and contemptible. Not a line have we from Council. I shall be much mistaken if the Observation of the Wise man will not be verified in some of them, that pride goeth before destruction and a haughty spirit before a fall. What the Conduct of Congress will be I cannot yet divine. Many of the members are heartily tired of this place and wish earnestly to remove. Yesterday they complained bitterly of being almost stewed and suffocated the night before in their small rooms. Duane seems averse to return. If he has any hopes of Congress fixing their residence in the state of NY, as he knows that will be agreeable to his state, he will sacrifice every consideration to gain popularity. It is a mortifying consideration that private and not public views too frequently influence the conduct of men at the helm of government. The common danger which has hitherto held these states together being now removed, I see local prejudices, passions and views already beginning to operate with all their force. And I confess I have my fears, that the predictions of our enemies will be found true, that on the removal of common danger our Confederacy & Union will be a rope of sand. There must & will undoubtedly be, for the sake of security, some confederation of states: But how many of the states will be comprehended in a Confederacy or how many confederacys there will be is yet uncertain. Were I to hazard a conjecture it would be that the

---

the course of which he had already served as a military secretary to Washington, member of Congress, and president of Pennsylvania. Though once political allies in Pennsylvania, Thomson and Reed had long been at odds because of their opposing views of the radical Pennsylvania constitution of 1776 and Reed's accusation that in 1778 Thomson had been party to an infringement of the state's sovereignty by an agent of Congress—a charge Thomson regarded as exaggerated and untimely. Reed did send to Princeton another address from the inhabitants of Philadelphia "with . . . emendations," but it mysteriously failed to reach Congress. See "Complaint of the Prest. & Council of Pensylva. ag. Congress," [1779], and Thomson to Reed, March 21, 1779, Charles Thomson Papers, Vol. ii, Library of Congress; Burnett, *Letters*, vii, 253; and John F. Roche, *Joseph Reed: A Moderate in the American Revolution* (New York, 1957).

four eastern states[2] will form one confederacy. Their manners, customs and governments are very similar And they are an unmixed people, being all sprung from a common stock without any great accession of strangers or foreigners. New Y will be compelled to join this confederacy either voluntarily or by force not from any of the causes aforementioned; But because the eastern states will not think themselves secure if Hudson's river & the northern lakes, which are the keys of the country, are kept by a people independent of and seperated from them. For this purpose the state of Vermont, which has hitherto given NY some trouble, will be supported & encouraged & kept as a rod over the head of N Y & if necessary used to chastise & compel it into the eastern Confederacy.[3] New Jersey, Pensylvania, Delaware and Maryland will form another Union. They are all states whose boundaries are fixed and confined and who have one common strong desire to possess a share of the great Western territory, which they now claim as their right and as an acquisition which the present confederacy has obtained by the expense of their blood and treasure.

The haughtiness of Virginia, its great extent and its boundless claims will induce it to set up for itself.[4] And if ever royal government is set up in N. America, here it will first erect its throne. Her first quarrel will be with the middle confederacy about the western Country. Unless perhaps the people beyond the Allegheny Mountains should be induced first to set up for themselves and to claim an exclusive right to that country. In that case Virginia may attempt to subjugate them & the middle confederacy will support them against her. She may then attempt to form an alliance with the Eastern confederacy or the three Southern states which it is not improbable may league together but without any close confederacy. For such is the fiery pride of South Carolina, such the dissipation of her morals & her insolence occasioned by the multitude of slaves that she will not cordially join in any Union till she is taught wisdom by sore suffering. In this conflict America may be a theatre of war & her councils become famous for brigues & intreagues of policy.

[2] Thomson used the phrase "eastern states" as a synonym for New England.
[3] Thomson first wrote "into the views of the eastern Confederacy" and then altered it to read as above.
[4] Thomson was undoubtedly hostile to Virginia's western claims at least in part because they included portions of his own state of Pennsylvania.

But where am I wandering. I sat down only to tell you I am well and am hurried on I know not how into scenes of fairy land from which I am recalled by Miss Nancy's invitation to breakfast. So I bid you Adieu. Take care of your health. I am, with sincere Affection, your loving husband

Cha Thomson

❖

Dear Hannah,   Saturday July 26. 1783
    What an astonishing change in the weather we have here since last evening! Yesterday we had a fresh breeze all day. But out of the current of air the heat was intollerable. About 3 o clock we had a gust of wind with a little rain. After that the breeze continued from the north west, & the heat of the weather was intense so that after dark we found it only tolerable, sitting in Col. Morgan's passage with both doors open. Yet this morning I am sitting in the front parlour with a cloath waiscoat under my gown, the windows down except one left a little up to change the air, the door shut, and I find my self comfortably cool. I hope you are careful to guard against those sudden changes. I received by Mr. Bond your agreeable letter dated Thursday morning. I am obliged to Mrs. D[1] for her attention to you & for the present she sent you. I would wish you not to suffer political conduct to break off social intercourse. True friendship is rare to be found; and few characters are perfect. But the intercourse of even civilities are agreeable. And virtues may be found, which will command esteem, in persons whose conduct we cannot always approve nay must sometimes severely condemn. You know how open a certain person[2] is to flattery & who, though he has shining parts, is not remarkable for solidity of judgement. His passions are too ungovernable and he is apt to suffer himself when under their influence to be the dupe of those who will flatter

RC (Princeton University Library: Charles Thomson Papers). Addressed: "Mrs. Thomson   Philadelphia   favoured by Mr Sterret."

[1] Mary Norris Dickinson, the wife of John Dickinson, was Hannah Thomson's cousin.
[2] John Dickinson.

his vanity. And yet he has many good qualities. I am much affraid that a young, sly & crafty politician,[3] of whose principles & conduct I have not the best Opinion, has found out his foible, and has had too much influence in the late transactions.

Nothing is yet done respecting the Address. We had no Congress yesterday. There were only six states in town, And I am apprehensive it will be the same to day. So that the business will rest till next week. I am inclined to think the report of the committee will not be much to my liking. I saw Duane & Williamson[4] yesterday in Consultation on the Address. They are two of the comee. They seemed to agree in Opinion & the latter seemed uncommonly pleased, which to me augurs no good, for I never knew him much pleased but when mischief was brewing, & in proportion to his pleasure I always judge of the degree of mischief. However I think there are so many of the members convinced of the impropriety of continuing here & of the impracticability of conducting the affairs of the Union in their present situation that they will either return back to Philada. or go home about their business. I shall stay till they come to some determination. Tell Page that Master & Bill Church are well, that B C in the beginning of the week eat too much green fruit & paid for it by being sick one day, that I ordered him to be fed next day with butter milk & charged him to eat no more green fruit which he observes & is now well and hearty. I am sorry poor Dick has lost his voice. I hope he will soon recover it & cheer his mistress with a song during my absence. Tell him one song to my charmer while I am absent will please me more than two to myself. My love to all friends.

I am with sincere affection, your loving husband

Cha Thomson

P.S. Mrs. Morgan & the children are well but the col. has got a

---

[3] This might be a reference to Alexander Hamilton, who had consulted with Dickinson on the measures the government of Pennsylvania intended to take against the Philadelphia mutineers and whose insistence that Dickinson's response to this crisis was ineffectual had been an important factor in Congress' decision to leave Philadelphia.

[4] Hugh Williamson (1735-1819), a Pennsylvania-born physician, merchant, and educator, graduated from the College of Philadelphia in 1757 and later received an M.D. from the University of Utrecht. After living in England for several years, Williamson moved to North Carolina in 1777 where he served

regular ague. Yesterday he shook & had a severe fever but which went off soon with a profuse sweat. After which he came down stairs. This is his well day. He is up and engaged in the business of his farm & intends with the assistance of a physician to ambuscade his enemy on his return & by the help of Ippecac & tar em[5] to spring a mine that will surprize the foe & then attack it vigorously with [cost. Joerw.?] by which he hopes to obtain a compleat victory. I heartily wish him success.

❖

Dear Hannah   Tuesday July 29 1783.

Yesterday the Commee. reported and Congress agreed to and passed an Answer to the address of the citizens. It turns out just as I suspected. D[1] has exerted his Cunning to gratify the malice of W,[2] and I dare say they value themselves on their skill & adroitness in waving the question of returning and passing over that part of the address which pointed to that. The address concludes with a solemn assurance "in testimony of the affections of the citizens to that Union, which has so happily succeeded in accomplishing the freedom and independence of America, that if either now or at any future time until the residence of Congress shall be permanently established it should appear to that honble. body that the situation of Philadelphia is convenient for transacting therein the concerns of the nation, *Congress may repose the utmost confidence in its*

---

as surgeon-general to the state's troops during the War for Independence and represented it in Congress for two terms—1782-85 and 1787-89. *DAB*.

[5] Widely prescribed in contemporary pharmacopoeias, tartar emetic was a medication for ague, considered to be an intermittent fever. Medical information courtesy of Professor Louis Landa.

RC (Princeton University Library: Charles Thomson Papers). Addressed: "Mrs. Thomson   Corner of Spruce and fourth Streets   Philadelphia."

[1] James Duane.
[2] Hugh Williamson.

*Inhabitants not only to prevent any circumstances, which may have a tend-
ency to disturb their necessary deliberations* but to aid in all measures
to support the national honor and dignity."

The committee with great circumspection has passed unnoticed
the former part of this solemn assurance & confined themselves
wholly to that contained in the last line. However as at courts compliments are used to supply the place of sincerity the answer is
drawn up in terms of great civility as follows.

"That the president inform the citizens of Philadelphia and its
liberties in answer to their *respectful & affectionate* Address that the
United States in Congress have *great satisfaction* in reviewing the
spirited and patriotic exertions which have been made by the government and citizens of Pensylvania in the course of the late glorious war and that they are highly pleased with the resolution
expressed by the citizens of Philadelphia to aid in all measures
which may have a tendency to support the national honor and
dignity."[3]

Mr. S. Huntington[4] arrived yesterday with his Collegue B. Huntington[5] from Connecticut, so that to day we shall have eight states
represented. These two have taken up their quarters in the stone
house at the foot of the hill beyond Col Morgan's cornfield. Mr.
Beresford[6] who has brought up his lady have taken a house below
Jug town. Thus are the members dispersed among the neigh-
bouring farm houses. How far they are in a situation to conduct
public business their works will manifest, and if in their present
situation they long preserve respect, I shall be greatly disappointed.

---

[3] This resolve, which was drafted by Hugh Williamson and approved by
Congress on July 28, 1783, is in *JCC*, xxiv, 452.

[4] Samuel Huntington (1731-96), a Connecticut lawyer and legislator who later
served as governor of the state, was a delegate to Congress for three terms
between 1775 and 1783 and president of that body from 1779 to 1781. See
Larry R. Gerlach, *Connecticut Congressman: Samuel Huntington, 1731-1796* (Hart-
ford, Conn., 1976).

[5] Benjamin Huntington (1736-1800), a graduate of Yale College, 1761, and
second cousin of Samuel Huntington, was a Connecticut lawyer and legislator
who was chosen to serve two terms in Congress—1780-83 and 1788. *Bio. Dir.
Cong.*

[6] Richard Beresford (1755-1803), a South Carolina planter and lawyer who
studied at the Middle Temple in London, spent a year in British captivity
during the War for Independence and was a member of Congress from 1783
to 1784. *Bio. Dir. Cong.*

I was invited to be of a party this evening at a tavern to dance & play cards. My answer was that I had resisted the allurements of Philadelphia and could not suffer myself to be drawn aside by the charms of Princeton.[7] I therefore hoped to be excused in not accepting the invitation. Some time ago a fellow stuck up an advertisement at a tavern door that he would entertain ladies and gentlemen with an exhibition of puppets, that would divert the company in three languages & that his next exhibition would be better than the last. Some of the members proposed as there were no other diversions in this place to entertain the ladies with a puppet show. I gravely answered that it would be well to consider how this would read in Oswald's next paper, in which they might expect to see this curious paragraph. "The public may be assured that the Congress of the U.S. are perfectly recovered from their late fright; for on —— evening last they entertained the ladies of Princeton with a puppet shew."

I long greatly to hear from you. I have not received a letter since that brought by Mr. Bond. I pray you to write to me as often as possible and take care of your health.

I am with sincere affection, Dear Hannah, your loving husband

Cha Thomson

[7] Thomson, whose stern republican virtue was proof against the temptations of Philadelphia and Princeton, easily succumbed to the blandishments of Annapolis, whither Congress moved after leaving Princeton. "Coming to the gay city of Annapolis where Pleasure holds her court," he wrote from the Maryland capital, "is it to be conceived that I, old & experienced as I am, could be so bad a courtier as not to conform to her customs. You will not therefore think it strange that I have attended Balls, plays & assemblies and that Mrs. T has had her tea parties dignified with the title of *Conversations*." See Thomson to George Clymer, April 3, 1784, Charles Thomson Papers, Vol. II, Library of Congress.

Dear Hannah   Wednesday July 30. 1783

I received by Mr. Remsen[1] your very agreeable letter dated Saturday and continued on till Monday. I was the more pleased as we had the most dismal accounts of the heat of the weather and of the mortality in Philadelphia. You will please to observe that I have written to you every morning except Sunday and dated my letters with the days of the week as well as of the month so that you will easily see whether all my letters have come to hand.

I have observed carefully all your cautions respecting my self and had pursued the measures recommended respecting William. I ordered him to write to his mother, but you know how slow he is in his motions. I question whether he will have his letter ready even to go with this. He is well. The house and lot you enquire about is Mr. Berrier's, on the left hand at the end of the town as you go to Mrs. Stockdens. I do not wonder at your not recollecting such a house as is described in the Advertisement. I assure you it appears very different on paper from what it is in reality. The description in the news paper reminds me of the Irishmans advertisement. His master missed a pair of yarn stocking, when he called his servant to account. The servant said they were lost or stolen but he would soon get them. How will you get them? I have advertised them. You rascal they are not worth the price of an Advertisement and will disgrace me if you have described them. O Master! I have taken care of that, I have advertised them as silk stockings.

I wish the general success, but I am afraid if he should carry his point, the soil is so old that it will yield little produce. You may tell Robert I am busily engaged in the study of Agriculture and preparing some directions for him in the management of his farm.[2]

RC (Princeton University Library: Charles Thomson Papers). Addressed: "Mrs. Thomson   the Corner of Spruce & 4 Streets   Philadelphia."

[1] Henry Remsen was a clerk in the office of secretary of Congress.

[2] The "directions" on agriculture Thomson was preparing for Robert McClenachan may have been the genesis of Thomson's *Notes on Farming* (New York, 1787), a compendium of practical advice for tillers of the soil that drew heavily on the early writings of Arthur Young, the noted English agriculturist,

Yesterday Mr. Hamilton called on his way home, so that for about an hour 9 states were represented in Congress. This short interval was improved to ratify the treaty with Sweden.[3] As soon as this was done he left Congress and proceeded on to his state so that we have now only 8 states in town. Not a word has yet been said of the return of Congress. Though every day's experience evinces that this is not a proper place. And the members are daily more & more convinced of it & their chagrin and vexation encrease. I am persuaded they will take up the matter soon—I think in the course of this week. I shall therefore wait the issue. Bond has given me notice that he intends to quit the Office as soon as Newyork is evacuated.[4] In the mean while he proposes to move his family to this place and has taken for them Mr. Morgan's house at the gate where the Office is now kept. For my own part I am determined to continue. I have contributed as much as in my power to erect the building & it shall tumble about my ears before I quit it. You

---

as well as on information received from Col. George Morgan of Princeton. Bee keeping was one of the subjects Thomson treated in his pamphlet, and in this regard it seems worth noting that among the Charles Thomson Papers held by Princeton University Library is a detached sheet containing a diagram of a bee house with the following remarks, which are not in Thomson's distinctive hand:

"Bee House—upon a scale of 1/2 an Inch to the foot—to contain 24 Hives of 9 Metres square and 8 Inches deep—each hive when filled will weigh 20 pounds—three hives of the same form and dimensions placed upon each other— the holes make the communication—the apertures to be 3 Inches long not more than 1/4 of an Inch wide—which prevents the mice from disturbing the Bees—The whole is perfectly close, except the small apertures in front—the rear is made entirely with doors upon hinges—to be secured in places of dangers with locks & bars."

[3] The treaty of amity and commerce that Benjamin Franklin signed with Sweden on April 3, 1783 was approved by Congress with only minor amendments. See Hunter Miller, ed., *Treaties and Other International Acts of the United States of America*, 8 vols. (Washington, D.C., 1931-48), II, 123-50. The diplomatic background of the treaty, which was the first to be concluded between the new American nation and a nonbelligerent power, is described in A. B. Benson, "Our First Unsolicited Treaty," *American Scandinavian Review*, VI (1919), 43-46.

[4] Congress accepted George Bond's resignation as its deputy secretary on October 30, 1783 and, with Thomson's support, awarded him $500 so that he could "retire from the service of his country with that decency which will become an officer of his character and trust in the United States." See *JCC*, XXV, 762; and Burnett, *Letters*, VII, 345, 372.

Alexander Hamilton by John Trumbull
Oil on canvas. Gift of the Avalon Foundation
Courtesy of the National Gallery of Art

have not said a word about Dick in your last. Has he recovered his voice? or is his harp still unstrung and hung on the willow? I hope Page, Cloe and Moll[5] are well. Please to tell Peter I expect he will rise a little sooner and not keep his Mistress so long without her breakfast. I shall consider any failure in my absence ten times greater than when I am at home & resent it accordingly. My love to all friends. Take care of your health.

I am with sincere affection, your loving husband

Cha Thomson

❖

Dear Hannah   Friday August 1. 1783.

The question for adjourning from this place is at length brought before Congress. It was yesterday moved by Mr. Read of S Carolina[1] in the words following:

"Resolved that on   the president shall adjourn Congress to meet at Philadelphia on   there to continue until the last Monday in October next, at which time the president shall adjourn Congress to meet at Annapolis on the friday following unless Congress shall before that time have determined otherwise."[2]

---

[5] Cloe and Moll were either servants or slaves of the Thomson family. See Robert McClenachan to Thomson, December 22, 1783, January 3 and 11, 1784, Charles Thomson Papers, Vol. i, Library of Congress.

RC (Princeton University Library: Charles Thomson Papers). Addressed: "Mrs. Thomson   at the Corner of Spruce & 4 Streets   Philadelphia."

[1] Jacob Read (1752-1816), a South Carolina lawyer who studied at Gray's Inn in London, served as a militia officer during the War for Independence and as a delegate to Congress from 1783 to 1785. *DAB.*

[2] Read's proposed resolution ironically produced a result directly opposite to the one he intended. David Howell of Rhode Island and Theodorick Bland of Virginia, who both opposed even a temporary return to Philadelphia, promptly took advantage of Read's resolution to urge the delegates on August 1 to approve an amended motion calling for Congress to adjourn from Princeton on August 8 and reconvene in Philadelphia on August 12, pending a decision in October 1783 on whether to move to Annapolis. Howell and Bland were

He prefaced his motion with observing that when Congress adjourned from Philada. it was generally understood by the house & it was particularly mentioned by the mover[3] and the members around him that it was only for a few days until the detachment from the army arrived to quell the mutineers; That had he not understood this to be the general sense of the house, he never would have consented to the adjournment. That every member must now be fully convinced that this was not a proper place for conducting public business; That even the members of Congress could not be provided with proper accommodations. That there were no conveniences for the Officers of Congress. That a minister was attending from the court of France, one was daily expected to arrive from Holland & others might be expected from other courts and here was no place for their reception or accommodation. That moreover the citizens of Philada. & the people of that State were extremely uneasy at the removal. That he would not mention what he had heard & what he knew, but he greatly feared that declining any longer to return would endanger the Union, affect the finances

---

confident that a majority of states would oppose this motion in the absence of a formal invitation from the government of Pennsylvania to return to the Quaker City, and in the event their confidence proved to be well founded. After delaying consideration of the Howell-Bland motion for almost two weeks, Congress rejected a slightly variant version of it on August 14 by a vote of six states to two, thereby effectively foreclosing any possibility that Congress would leave Princeton and return to Philadelphia. JCC, XXIV, 484-85, 506. Howell and Bland joined the majority in voting against their own motion, prompting a somewhat bemused Virginia delegate who arrived in Congress shortly after the crucial vote on the 14th to report to James Madison: "The Question for the return to Phila. had been decided in the negative prior to my arrival. I must think a worthy colleague [Theodorick Bland] hurried this matter on with an unbecoming precipitation, & I am at a loss to reconcile with his professed candor & openness, his making a motion with an intention of voting agt. it, supported by Mr. Howell the inventer of this ingenious & Honourable device." See John Francis Mercer to Madison, [August 14, 1783], William T. Hutchinson et al., eds., *The Papers of James Madison*, 14 vols. (Chicago, Ill., and Charlottesville, Va., 1962-), VII, 277. Since Thomson was in Philadelphia between August 9 and 18, he was unable to witness most of these intricate parliamentary maneuvers.

[3] Thomson is probably referring to Alexander Hamilton, who was the author of the crucial committee report advising Congress to leave Philadelphia in the wake of the mutiny of the Pennsylvania Line.

& ruin the credit of the United states. He hoped therefore his motion would be seconded & meet the approbation of the house. He then sat down and a long silence ensued. I dare not trust myself in describing the countenances of some individuals during this interval of silence, or the various passions with which they were visibly actuated, notwithstanding their utmost care to conceal them. It was a sight worthy the notice of the Athenian, who had learned by careful observation to trace accurately the passions of the Soul by the lines of the Countenance and whose skill Plato, Zenophon and the rest of the disciples of Socrates admired, while their master bore witness to the truth of it. I will confess that had he fixed his Eyes on me while I was viewing the countenances of some, he would have seen a gush of indignation too visible to be concealed. At length Mr. McHenry of Maryland arose.[4] He said he had looked round and waited to hear the motion seconded. It certainly deserved the attention of the house. In his opinion much depended on the determination of it, nothing less than the peace of a great & important state & perhaps that of the Union. That it was high time the subject should be taken into consideration. He therefore seconded the motion, & hoped it would be seriously considered before a vote was taken.

Mr. Williamson moved to commit the motion; this was opposed. It was then moved to Assign a day for the consideration of it, this also met with Opposition and the debates continued till at last an adjournment was called for and agreed to, so that by that means the subject was put off till next day. It was curious to observe with what care the speakers endeavoured to conceal their sentiments and the votes they meant to give. I expect the subject will be resumed to day, but I question much whether they will come to a decision this week.[5]

[4] James McHenry (1753-1816), John Adams' secretary of war, was an Irish immigrant who studied medicine with Dr. Benjamin Rush, served in the Continental Army as a military surgeon as well as secretary to Washington, and represented Maryland in Congress from 1783 to 1785. See Bernard C. Steiner, *The Life and Correspondence of James McHenry* (Cleveland, 1907). Unlike Howell and Bland, McHenry and Read did vote to adjourn Congress to Philadelphia.

[5] This paragraph clearly indicates that Thomson wrote this letter early in the morning of August 1, before Congress reconvened to consider the resolution for an adjournment to Philadelphia offered by Read on July 31.

Adieu my dear Hannah. Take care of your health. I am with sincere affection, your loving husband

Cha Thomson

Please to forward the enclosed. Mrs. M & family send their love to you.

Dear Hannah,   Tuesday. August 19. 1783

I arrived safe yesterday about half after 10.[1] As we had several showers on the road I was very uneasy about you. If the showers reached you, I hope you took care to have the apron up and the curtains drawn. I shall be anxious to hear from you.

I find the president is not likely to find a house. He had cast his eyes on the house where Mr. Smith lives, which it seems belongs to the president of the College.[2] Some intimation was given to the P. that doct. Witherspoon would rent this house as he lived in his own house.[3] Whether the doctor from a laudable desire of improving his income had it in contemplation to turn out his son-in-

RC (Princeton University Library: Charles Thomson Papers). Addressed: "Mrs. Thomson   Corner of Spruce and 4 Streets   Philada."

[1] Thomson had been in Philadelphia since August 9, visiting his wife and transacting official business relating to the ratification of the treaty with Sweden and the peacetime military establishment. See Burnett, *Letters*, VII, 256-57.

[2] Samuel Stanhope Smith (1751-1819), a Presbyterian minister and educator who was a graduate of the College of New Jersey, 1769, was currently Professor of Moral Philosophy and Theology at the College and later served as its seventh president from 1795 to 1812. Smith, who was also the son-in-law of President Witherspoon, resided in the President's House of the College at this time. *Princetonians*, II, 42-51.

[3] John Witherspoon (1723-94), who served as sixth president of the College of New Jersey from 1768 to 1794 and represented New Jersey in Congress between 1776 and 1782, was living at Tusculum, a home he owned about a mile from the College. An old print of Tusculum is reproduced in Varnum L. Collins, *President Witherspoon: A Biography*, 2 vols. (Princeton, 1925), I, facing p. 147. Contrary to Thomson's expectations, Witherspoon did not rent the President's House to Elias Boudinot, and thereafter the president of Congress was apparently unable to find satisfactory accommodations in Princeton. See *JCC*, XXV, 532n1.

John Witherspoon by Charles Willson Peale
Oil on canvas
Courtesy of Independence National Historical Park Collection

law & daughter & rent the house to the Pr. for a high rent, or whether any drew that conclusion from the prevailing temper of the doctr. I will not undertake to say, but the P. without farther ceremony applied to Mr. Smith & informed him that he understood Mr. W intended to rent the house. This was a thunder clap to Mr. S. He said he had heard nothing of the matter. Mr. W had not mentioned it to him. He did not know where to go with his family. He had put himelf to inconvenience to accommodate Members as much as he could. But he supposed he must give up his house. Possibly the trustees might think they had a right to let it as the presidt. of the College did not live in it himself. You can easily judge the feelings on both sides.[4]

I am, your affectionate husband

Cha Thomson

[4] Thomson wrote another letter to his wife on August 21, 1783 of which only the following extract, taken from the Edmund C. Burnett Papers, Library of Congress, has been found:

"I have received your letters dated Monday 12 o'clock and Tuesday 10 o'clock at night and acknowledged the receipt of them. . . . Mr. Read was misinformed respecting the adjournment. They met on Monday but they might as well have adjourned till this time for any business they have done. I am very apprehensive that nothing but some calamity will awaken the states to a sense of their situation. . . .

"The President of Congress has not provided a house for himself nor is [it] likely he will find one here to suit him. I find Elizabethtown has been talked of at his table as a proper place for the residence of Congress. He has a house there which he says has twenty rooms and which he will let for the use of the President. It is true the place is infested with mosquitoes in summer and lying low and near marshes may be liable to intermittents in the spring and fall, but these are trifling when it is considered that by fixing the residence of Congress there the value of his estate will be increased and he will have an opportunity of letting his house at a good rent. But yet I am inclined to believe this will be opposed by his colleagues; for Mr. Condi[c]t has found a lodging in this town at 3 dollars a week which enables him to lay up money. And there is reason to fear that at Elizabethtown, which is so near New York, it will cost him at least four. This would be a clear loss of 52 dollars a year which is no trifling consideration, and which I daresay will have due weight with some others. There are other weighty considerations which might be mentioned."

President Boudinot's talk about luring Congress to Elizabethtown, N.J., was not idle chatter. In response to Boudinot's prompting, Gen. Elias Dayton was already busy procuring an address from the people of Elizabethtown offering their town as a meeting place for Congress. This address arrived in Congress on August 23, 1783, but despite Boudinot's best efforts the delegates did nothing more than express their gratitude to Elizabethtown for the offer. See *JCC*, xxv, 548; and Burnett, *Letters*, vii, 250-51.

◆

Dear Hannah   Wednesday Aug 27 1783

Yesterday I received your letter No. 1. and acknowledged the rect. of that dated Friday.

The general had his Audience.[1] I must inform you that before he arrived the etiquette for receiving him was settled as follows.

"The general on receiving his Audience shall be introduced (it ought to have been expressed the General shall be introduced to his Audience) by two members & placed in a chair near and on the right hand of the president. The President to be covered and to speak to the general in his seat, and to receive his address sitting. The members of each state during the conference to sit together & keep their seats, uncovered as usual. The two first members present of the committee appointed to confer with him are to introduce the general."[2]

The members being all seated and the President having heightened his seat [with] a large folio to give him an elevation above the rest, the general was introduced & upon entering the room bowed to the president & then to the members on the right & left who all returned the bow sitting. He was then conducted to his chair, but upon being addressed by the president he arose & stood while the president read the speech that had been prepared. As soon as it was finished, he made a reply & having finished he bowed to the president & members and immediately withdrew. I enclose a copy of the speech and the reply for your satisfaction. When you have read them please to seal them up and send them to Claypole as directed.[3]

RC (Princeton University Library: Charles Thomson Papers). Addressed: "Mrs. Thomson   Corner of Spruce & 4 Streets   Philadelphia."

[1] Congress had summoned Washington to meet with it at Princeton so that the delegates could formally tender their thanks to him for his leadership during the War for Independence and confer with him on the peacetime military establishment. For further information on the latter issue, see Charles Thomson to Hannah Thomson, October 24, 1783.
[2] Elias Boudinot and James Duane devised the etiquette for Congress' reception of Washington, which took place on August 26, 1783. JCC, XXIV, 522n.
[3] President Boudinot's speech to Washington, which was drafted by James Wilson of Pennsylvania, and Washington's reply are in JCC, XXIV, 521-23. They

Mr. Jones[4] & Mr. Madison[5] arrived yesterday afternoon. They inform me to my great satisfaction that our Assembly are proceeding with great wisdom and moderation & that they have determined to adopt the measures recommended by Congress for discharging the debts and supporting the honor and credit of the United states.[6] This is not only sound wisdom & policy but it will be taking a noble revenge of those who wished to provoke them to rash measures. I am confident there are some who will be deeply wounded by this conduct, and I shall rejoice in proportion to the keenness of the pangs they feel.

I really cannot form any opinion about the return of Congress. If public good or private convenience governed the votes of all the members it would be easy to form a judgment. I wish most sincerely to fall upon some plan that will make the time pass more agreeably to us both. You may be assured that the visit you mention was planned before & without any knowledge of or view to present circumstances. It was to avoid the rage of the dog star: as soon as that sets which will be next monday week the visitant returns. I shall with great pleasure meet you at Bristol & have a room prepared for your reception. You will please to drive up to Bassonets.

---

were published in the August 30, 1783 issue of David C. Claypoole's *Pennsylvania Packet; or, The General Advertiser.*

[4] Joseph Jones (1727-1805), a Virginia lawyer, jurist, and state legislator who was educated at the Inner Temple and the Middle Temple in London, served two terms in Congress—1777-78 and 1780-83. *DAB.*

[5] James Madison (1751-1836), Virginia planter, statesman, and fourth president of the United States, was a graduate of the College of New Jersey, 1771, who served in Congress from 1780 to 1783 and from 1787 to 1788. His first term in Congress has been freshly analyzed in Lance Banning, "James Madison and the Nationalists, 1780-1783," *William and Mary Quarterly*, 3d ser., XL (1983), 227-55. Despite having lived for three years in Princeton, Madison considered it an unsuitable meeting place for Congress because of its "unfitness for transacting the public business" and "deficiency of accomodation." William T. Hutchinson et al., eds., *The Papers of James Madison*, 14 vols. (Chicago, Ill., and Charlottesville, Va., 1962-), VII, 379.

[6] For the favorable resolutions adopted by the Pennsylvania Assembly in reponse to Congress' comprehensive plan of April 18, 1783 for paying the public debt and securing for itself a limited right of taxation, see *JCC*, XXIV, 526-27. The Pennsylvania delegates undoubtedly submitted these resolutions to Congress with the hope of inducing the delegates to reconsider their decision not to return to Philadelphia.

I am much pleased with Robert's present plan & future prospects: so far from thinking him whimsical I consider him as a prudent man, fixed in his purpose to provide for his family and accommodating himself to circumstances as they arise. I think he would be to blame if he refused so advantageous an offer. It has my hearty approbation & I sincerely wish him success.

I thank you for your care of me and shall be much obliged for the jacket. What an amazing change in the weather! I am told you had a plentiful rain on Monday evening. We had none here. The wind was high and the lightening though distant appeared to be very sharp.

I desired Bond, if he had occasion to go to the office, to call for the key; but I think it would have been best to have brought it back & left it with you. He passed through this place yesterday on his way to New york. As the passengers dine at Brunswick, his stay was so short that I did not see him. William proceeds in his snail pace of copying. I have not had an Opportunity of examining his performances the two days past. But I think he will improve as much as if he were with Tod. We had heard of the death of Galloway but not of the marriage of his daughter.[7] I would not wish her as much disappointment as her father experienced but if she be happy it will be more than she deserves.

Adieu my dear Hannah, take care of your health. I am with sincere affection, your loving husband

Cha Thomson

[7] Despite rumors of his demise, the noted Pennsylvania Loyalist Joseph Galloway, who had left America in 1778 never to return, was destined to endure twenty more years of exile in England before his death in 1803. *DAB*. Thomson's vengeful attitude toward Galloway's reported death doubtless stemmed from the fact that the two men had been bitter political adversaries in Pennsylvania even before Galloway elected to side with the British following Congress' rejection of his famous Plan of Union in 1774.

❖

Dear Hannah,   Thursday Septr. 4. 1783

I have received your letter of Monday N. 4 and am glad to hear of your welfare and of your prudent precaution to guard against the sudden change of the weather. I am told there has been a frost on the north side of the hills round this town. We find a fire not only comfortable but necessary. I delivered William the letter you enclosed, but Page had been so careful in sealing it that it cost him a great deal of trouble to open it and after all his pains when it was opened it turned out like the three last days debates in a certain house—just nothing. I have directed W to prepare an Answer and have it ready to go by this opportunity. I wish to promote the correspondence, as I am inclined to think the correspondence between William and Page and the Journals of Princeton,[1] should they descend to posterity, will be equally improving and diverting.

Mr. Wright informs me he has begun the bust of the general. I hope he will succeed. He is to paint both the general and his Lady.[2]

Give my respects to cousin N. Lloyd. I hope she will spend some days with you. I slept so long this morning that I can only assure you that I am, with sincere affection, yr.

Cha Thomson

RC (Princeton University Library: Charles Thomson Papers). Addressed: "Mrs. Thomson   Corner of Spruce & 4 Streets   Philadelphia."

[1] That is, the journals of the proceedings of Congress during its stay in Princeton.

[2] Joseph Wright (1756-93), a portrait painter from New Jersey, was the son of the noted modeler in wax Patience Lovell Wright and a pupil of the celebrated artist Benjamin West. Wright painted portraits of General and Mrs. Washington during their stay at Rocky Hill, N.J., in the fall of 1783, and the commander in chief was so impressed by the quality of Wright's artistry that in the following year he praised the New Jerseyan's portrait of him as "a better likeness of me than any other painter has done." See Fiske Kimball, "Joseph Wright and His Portraits of Washington," *Antiques*, xv (1929), 377-82. Unfortunately the young artist enjoyed less success in fashioning a bust of Washington that was designed to serve as a model for a European sculptor who was to be employed by Congress to create an equestrian statue of the general. After having obliged the hapless Washington to lay "on his back, with his face covered with the wet plaster" for a long period of time, Wright accidentally broke the plaster cast while removing it from the general's face, whereupon the indignant Virginian refused "to comply with the wishes of Congress so far as to undergo

Dear Hannah   Friday Sept 12 1783
   I received your letter dated Wednesday 9 o Clock, and am highly
pleased with your arrangements with the Black family, so that there
will be no occasion of sending the notice which I enclosed in my
letter of yesterday,[1] and the present tenant may take time to look
out for another place.
   I have received a letter from Madeira with a bill of lading for
my pipe of wine which is arrived at Philadelphia in the brig Olive
Branch capt John Brice. I enclose you the bill of Lading that you
may request our cousin Robert or Jonathan to get it on shore. I
could wish the porters would get some boards to save the stairs
and try to put it in the store room. Where if the cask is good as I
expect it is it may stand on the end and take up but little room.
   I find by the letter that the fine tale of the Prest. either originated
in his sanguine temper or that it was fabricated merely to gain
custom. However if the wine be good as I hope it is I am glad I
sent for it; but I find I shall be six or seven pounds sterling in debt
for it over and above my 22 bbls of flour. There will be 40/ to be
paid for the freight and I suppose something for duty on impor-
tation which you will please to furnish.
   It is uncertain whether I shall have the pleasure of seeing you
on Saturday. This days debate may determine it; though I am
apprehensive nothing will be decided. Fitzsimmons & Montgomery[2]
arrived yesterday & Jones & Madison are expected to day. We have

another prostration." See William Dunlap, *A History of the Rise and Progress of
the Arts of Design in the United States*, ed. Frank W. Bayley and Charles E. Good-
speed, 3 vols. (Boston, 1918-25), I, 371-72.

RC (Princeton University Library: Charles Thomson Papers). Addressed:
"Mrs. Thomson   Corner of Spruce & 4 Streets   Philadelphia."

   [1] This letter has not been found.
   [2] John Montgomery (1722-1808), an Irish immigrant who became a Pennsylvania soldier, state legislator, and jurist, served in Congress from 1782 to
1784.

James Madison by James Sharples
Pastel. The Art Museum, Princeton University

received a warm invitation from the inhabitants of Germantown to fix upon that place for the permanent residence of Congress. They offer their public school for the accommodation of Congress and the public Offices, & give assurances that the members shall be well provided with houses.[3]

I am glad to find Page remembers his friends, But am sorry to hear nothing of poor Dick.

Adieu my dear Hannah. I am with sincere affection, your loving husband

Cha Thomson

Dear Hannah,   Saturday Septr. 13 1783.

Yesterday the president returned and brought with him the dispatches which came by the Washington Packet, which were so voluminous that the whole day was Spent in reading them;[1] So that the subject about which you are so anxious to hear was not taken up, and whether it will be the subject of this day's debate is altogether Uncertain. There are now ten states represented. But Delaware is still absent. Every day demonstrates & exhibits new proofs of the impropriety & inconveniency of continuing here. But when or where they will move is a subject on which I can form no judgment for reasons mentioned in my former letters.

---

[3] The "invitation" to use Germantown, Pa., as a permanent meeting place for Congress, dated September 4, signed by over 400 residents, and received by Congress on September 11, 1783, is in PCC, item 46, fols. 117-21. The delegates probably took no official notice of this offer because of Germantown's close proximity to Philadelphia.

RC (Princeton University Library: Charles Thomson Papers). Addressed: "Mrs. Thomson   Corner of Spruce & 4 Streets   Philadelphia."

[1] These "dispatches" consisted of about thirty letters from American diplomats and diplomatic agents in Europe, the earliest dated April 7 and the latest July 27, 1783. See Francis Wharton, ed., *The Revolutionary Diplomatic Correspondence of the United States*, 6 vols. (Washington, D.C., 1889), VI, 364, 368, 373-74, 432-33, 455-56, 464-65, 477, 494-570, 576, 580-91, 600-606.

I am glad we did not conclude to meet this day at Bristol as Congress have agreed to sit.

I received no letter by yesterdays stage but hope for the pleasure of one to day.

Adieu, dear H, take care of your health. I am with sincere affection, your loving husband

Cha Thomson

P.S. I enclose a sheet of Williams writing, it is not quite so good as his last, but it serves as a letter for Page.

Dear Hannah   Saturday Evening Septr. 13. 1783

I just write to inform you that the day passed without any consideration of the question about adjournment. They have however agreed to accept the cession made by Virginia of their claim to the country on the west side of the Ohio.[1] So that some public business has been done. I have recd. your two letters and am glad to hear Dick has got his voice.

I am with sincere affection, your loving husband

Cha Thomson

RC (Princeton University Library: Charles Thomson Papers). Addressed: "Mrs. Thomson   Philadelphia   favoured by Mr. Fitzsimmons."

[1] The conditions Congress laid down this day for accepting Virginia's cession of all the lands she claimed northwest of the Ohio and Congress' approval on March 1, 1784 of a new deed of cession drawn up by Virginia in accordance with these terms brought into being the national domain and set the stage for the passage of the Land Ordinance of 1785 and the Northwest Ordinance of 1787, which enunciated basic principles for the government and administration of the American territorial system that remained in force even after the adoption of the Federal Constitution. Thomson discussed the significance of the Virginia cession at length in his September 15, 1783 letter to his wife.

Dear Hannah   Monday Sept 15. 1783

I received your very agreeable letters of thursday & friday N. 9 & 10. I am extremely sorry that I cannot yet give you any flattering hopes of the speedy return of Congress. They all are sensible of the inconvenience of this place; they all acknowledge it. But one drawing one way and another, another, they are kept still here, which only breeds more ill humours & keeps the members, and all concerned with them, in a constant fret. The hopes that some had of gratifying their malice and reaking their vengeance on the Superin.[1] are I fancy somewhat abated though the inclination and desire continue as strong as ever. In their last attack they were handled with great freedom, and the ringleader[2] was drawn to solemn asseverations that he was not influenced by personal resentments, but by public motives; though I fancy he was convinced that few believed him.

On Saturday last they agreed to accept on certain terms the cession made by Virginia to the United States of the claims of that state to all the lands beyond the Ohio. This will give a great weight to the authority of Congress. It gives them the sovereignty and property of a country at least five hundred miles square. And whether they make the best use of it or not, I hope it will lay the foundations of liberty still broader by the separate jurisdictions and states that will be erected in that bounds. For by the articles of acceptance they bind themselves to lay it out into distinct and separate states of 150 or 200 miles square or as near thereto as circumstances will admit, and that each of those states shall be members of the fœderal Union and intitled to all the benefits of it. Some

RC (Princeton University Library: Charles Thomson Papers). Addressed: "Mrs. Thomson   corner of Spruce & 4 Streets   Philadelphia."

[1] Robert Morris.

[2] This was almost certainly the perennially suspicious Arthur Lee of Virginia, whose deep-rooted conviction that Robert Morris was personally corrupt led him to charge about this time that under the superintendent of finance's tenure "the public money is lavishd away, the Soldiery defrauded and the public plunderd." Burnett, *Letters,* VII, 300. In addition, Lee had recently offered motions calling for congressional investigations of certain aspects of Morris' official conduct. *JCC,* XXV, 536-37, 541-43.

have it in idea to make this country a fund to discharge the debt contracted by the war. The army first to have the lands promised them and so much of the remainder to be sold or assigned to public creditors as will discharge the debt. Maryland & Jersey however are not yet satisfied. They think that all the country which lies beyond the Allegheny Mountains and which was unsettled at the commencement of the war and which belonged to the crown of GB & was by it ceded to the United states in the articles of the peace ought to be thrown into a common stock and disposed of for the benefit of the union. They think that Virginia, the Carolinas and Georgia have no right in virtue of antiquated charters to a country gained by the blood & treasure and by the common exertions of the whole. And in this they have a great deal of reason & justice on their side. However I am pleased that so much is like to be peaceably obtained.

Adieu my dear Hannah. I am with sincere affection, your loving husband

Cha Thomson

My dear Hannah   Tuesday Septr. 16. 1783.

I am now inclined to believe you were right in your conjecture that those who do not wish to return to Philadelphia will while away the time till the first Monday in October the day assigned for considering of a proper place for the permanent residence of Congress.[1] I find now that when they are asked why they do not decide upon the place proper for the temporary residence of Congress which was agreed to be done on friday last[2] the answer is that the time for determining on the permanent residence is so near that

RC (Princeton University Library: Charles Thomson Papers). Addressed: "Mrs. Thomson   Corner of Spruce & 4 Streets   Philadelphia."

[1] Congress had decided as early as June 4, 1783 to set aside the first Monday in October of that year for considering the issue of a permanent meeting place. JCC, XXIV, 381-82.

[2] Although it is clear from other sources that Congress met on Friday, September 12, 1783, there is no record of its proceedings on that day in JCC.

it is not worth while to trouble themselves about a temporary residence until that is decided.

Yesterday was taken up in a most curious debate. A foreigner, a native of the east Indies had entered our service as a sailor in 1778 or 1779. He had served on board the Bon Homme Richard under Capt J. P. Jones and in the celebrated action with the Serapis had lost a leg, by which he is disabled from procuring a living. He and two others in like condition had applied more than a twelve month ago to obtain something to support them. His request not having been complied with this poor stranger came to this town and presented himself to the members. The remembrance of the gallant action performed, his maimed condition, distressed looks and modest deportment naturally raised compassion and yesterday his case was considered. Had he been a citizen of any of the United states, he would have been comprehended under an Act which passed in 1776 and which granted to such objects half pay for life. But being a stranger and foreigner he had nothing to rest on but the bounty and Compassion of Congress. And unfortunately for him Mr. Morris as agent of marine had recommended that he should be paid a pension of 40 dollars a year during his life. This recommendation was sufficient to excite the opposition of those whose malice seems so inveterate that they would risque their salvation to ruin the man & trample on every feeling of humanity & violate every law of Justice to gratify their resentment. However after a great deal of debate which consumed the day in spite of the opposition of Higgenson,[3] Bland and Ellery, the grant was made, and the poor fellows prevented from starving in our streets after having lost their limbs in our service.[4]

I have received your letter of Sunday N 11. I am very sorry for your disappointment which accounts to me for your not being in a pleasant humour. I thank Dick most heartily for his politeness and complaisance in endeavouring to solace his mistress with a song & to charm her into good humour by his warbling notes. I hope

[3] Stephen Higginson (1743-1820) was a Massachusetts merchant who served in Congress from 1782 to 1783. *DAB*.

[4] This day Congress awarded annual pensions of $40 to Joseph Brussels, John Jordan, and James McKinsey, "ordinary seamen in the navy of the United States," who had been seriously maimed during the *Bonhomme Richard's* famous engagement with H.M.S. *Serapis* in September 1779. *JCC*, xxv, 568-69.

Page rewarded him with at least two spiders. I approve your Arrangements respecting the wine. Enclosed I send you for your amusement a medal invented by Doct. Franklin & which he has had struck as a lasting monument of the capture of Burgoyne & Cornwallis and of the important aids afforded to America by her great and generous benefactor.[5]

I am my dear Hannah, with most sincere affection, your loving husband

Cha Thomson

Dear Hannah   Wednesday Sept 17. 1783

Another day is passed in disputations which though they did not wound the feelings of humanity as those of the day before, yet excited no less indignation, being founded on ignorance as well as malice. In 1781 an Arrangement had been formed for the marine department with a secretary at the head of it whose salary was fixed at 4000 dollars a year. To this office major genl. McDougal[1] was elected, but he declined accepting it unless he might retain his rank in the army. And this not being agreed, the election became void. The arrangement was then changed and an Agent of marine was

---

[5] The *Libertas Americana* medal commemorating American victories at Saratoga and Yorktown was devised by Benjamin Franklin in conjunction with two French medalists—Augustin Dupre and E. A. Gibelin. Heavily influenced by the classical tradition of which Thomson himself was an ardent admirer, the medal portrayed an infant Hercules strangling two serpents while Minerva shielded him from an attacking leopard. These figures represented in turn the fledgling American nation, her faithful French ally, and their perfidious British foe. See Carl Zigrosser, "The Medallic Sketches of Augustin Dupre in American Collections," American Philosophical Society, *Proceedings*, CI (1957), 535-50.

RC (Princeton University Library: Charles Thomson Papers). Addressed: "Mrs. Thomson   Corner of Spruce & 4 Streets   Philadelphia."

[1] Alexander McDougall (1732-86), the noted New York merchant, revolutionary leader, and Continental Army officer, served two terms in Congress— 1781-82 and 1784-85. DAB.

to be placed at the head of it with a salary of 1500 dollars a year; but not being able to fix on a person to fill the Office Congress resolved that until an Agent of marine could be appointed, the duties of his Office should be devolved on & executed by the Superintendant of finance.[2]

A remonstrance was lately received from the legislature of Massachusetts complaining of the expense of the civil list.[3] This afforded a favourable opportunity to the junto. For finding the Superintendt. in the exercise of the duties of Agent of marine and not remembering or knowing what was passed, they thought he was the agent and intitled to the salary in addition to what he received as Superint. and that by abolishing the office they would not only lessen his dignity but also lower his income. Bland had a few days before violently opposed the sale of the frigate alliance: He then saw the necessity of having a marine force and hoped the U.S. would never lose sight of it; He observed and with reason that the time of peace was the time for laying the foundation of a marine without which it was impossible for them[4] to be a commercial nation or to be respectable at home or abroad. But now the Super. being held up to his view all this fine reasoning was forgotten, & the house was dinned with the absurdity of continuing an Agent when we had no navy. This wise debate consumed the day, and nothing was done.[5]

I had not the pleasure of hearing from you yesterday. I am informed that it is sickly in town. I hope you are careful of your health. I purpose being down on Saturday and shall bring William with me.

I am with sincere affection, Dear Hannah, your loving husband
Cha Thomson

[2] There is a concise description of Robert Morris' tenure as agent of the marine, to which office he was appointed on September 7, 1781, in Clarence L. Ver Steeg, *Robert Morris: Revolutionary Financier. With an Analysis of His Earlier Career* (Philadelphia, 1954), 71-72.

[3] See Charles Thomson to Hannah Thomson, September 18, 1783, note 5.

[4] Thomson first wrote "for the U.S." and then altered it to read as above.

[5] Robert Morris continued to serve as agent of the marine until his resignation as superintendent of finance in 1784.

My dear Hannah,   Thursday Sept. 18. 1783

Another day is spent in ill humour and fruitless debates. The subject was to satisfy the Eastern states & reconcile them to the commutation agreed to be given to the Officers in lieu of the half pay that had been promised them. You know that in the midst of the war, when the army was exposed to hunger and nakedness, and their pay was reduced to a trifle by the depreciation of the paper money or, according to the phrase then in vogue, by the advanced price of the necessaries of life, the officers became discontented and wanted to resign. In Order to satisfy them, the Congress at York town[1] agreed that such as continued in service to the end of the war should be intitled to and receive after the war was over their full pay for seven years, provided they lived so long. The benefit of this was afterwards extended to the widows & children of such as died in the service. Still however the army was discontented. They wanted a provision for life; that after wearing out their constitution in the service of their country they might not, in their old age, be exposed to want and misery. The continent was much divided on this subject. The eastern states were in general averse to it, as it seemed to encourage the idea of a standing army, the other states favoured the measure. It was long a subject of debate. At length however, our finances being exhausted, our affairs gloomy, the discontents of the army encreasing, and assurances being given that this would satisfy them, & it appearing to be the only means in the power of Congress to prevent a dissolution of the army, some of the eastern states gave way and in Sept 1780 Congress resolved that such of the officers as continued in service to the end of the war should be intitled to half pay for life. But though the eastern states from the necessity of the case agreed to the measure, the genius or prejudices of the people were against it, and therefore the officers saw that they could not enjoy that bounty with peace and satisfaction. You know what influence a

RC (Princeton University Library: Charles Thomson Papers).

[1] That is, York, Pa., where Congress met from September 1777 to June 1778 during the British occupation of Philadelphia.

word has upon the passions of the people. The word *pension* which conveyed an Odious idea was applied to the half pay, and a cry was raised, that the conclusion of the war would saddle the country with a band of *pensioners*. The merit and sufferings of the army were acknowledged, and it was alledged and asserted that the people would readily agree to give them an ample compensation; but that they could not agree to pay them annually a sum for life, which would only encourage idleness and dissipation and create an odious distinction among the citizens. To obviate all objections the officers at the close of last campaign offered to receive a sum in gross in lieu of the half pay promised. This was one of the objects of the deputation from the army last fall.[2] After long debates and strong symptoms of a most dangerous mutiny in the whole army, it was at last agreed by Congress, that the Officers should be entitled to the value of five years full pay as a commu[ta]tion for the half pay; that all their accounts and claims should be liquidated & settled, and that certificates should be given to each of them for the balance due including the commutation; that this should be funded with the general debt of the nation; and that the interest thereof should be paid annually until the principal could be discharged. And Congress proceeded to call upon the states to grant and establish funds for the regular payment of the interest and discharge of the principal of the whole national debt. The states to the eastward, it seems, are dissatisfyed with this arrangement, and the legislature of Massachusetts has remonstrated to Congress against the allowance to the army and the expence of the civil list. This remonstrance was referred to a committee, who reported an Answer with reasons to shew that Congress could not, consistent with public faith, honor, justice and humanity, make any alteration in the commutation, but that they were disposed as far as was consistent with the public good to reduce the expences of the civil list. This report not being

---

[2] Thomson first wrote "in January last" and then changed it to "last fall." He was probably alluding to the famous Newburgh Conspiracy in which a coalition of nationalist political leaders in and out of Congress and discontented army officers combined to raise the specter of an army mutiny in order to compel Congress to approve plans for a federal tax on imports and pensions for military officers. See Richard H. Kohn, "The Inside History of the Newburgh Conspiracy: America and the Coup d'Etat," *William and Mary Quarterly*, 3d ser., xxvii (1970), 187-220.

satisfactory to the eastern delegates was committed to three of them who brought in another report which has engaged the attention of Congress for these two days past, and is likely to engage it for some time to come. The report began with a proposal to abolish the marine department or at least reduce it to an Agent with a triffling salary. This afforded a favourable opportunity to those who wished to have a stroke at the Superint. of finance, who they conceived was the agent & received the emoluments. And as every subject wherein he is concerned is agitated with great warmth & bitterness, this employed the whole of the first day. Yesterday what regarded the civil list was referred to a new committee, and the latter part of the report which related to the commutation was taken into consideration. The report proposed that Congress should pass a resolution, by which the states should be left to settle with the Officers of their respective lines on the best terms they could and to take up the certificates given to the officers & have them discounted at the public treasury in discharge of the requisitions of Congress. This was opposed as a measure tending to violate the public faith pledged to the officers, to throw them upon the mercy of the states and to deprive them of the hard and well earned rewards of their meritorious services. It was supported on the other hand as necessary to the peace and tranquility of the states and to the preservation of the Union. Read opposed it with great warmth, McHenry & Madison with great force of reason & argument. Holten[3] who was in favour of the measure & who is a worthy good man but of weak nerves seemed to be deeply affected with apprehensions of the consequences, urged it with great seriousness & deep Concern, pointing out the dangers & deprecating the evil consequences that might ensue from a refusal. Ellery, who was also in favour of it, and who has a predominant passion to be thought a wit, and whose wit indeed, though far from being acute or refined, much surpasses his judgment or honesty, endeavoured to represent the half pay as extorted from the fears of Congress; and as he scorns to confine his fancy within the bounds of truth, he boldly attempted to impose on the members by the grossest falsehoods, in which however he was immediately detected. But to cover his

[3] Samuel Holten (1738-1816), a Massachusetts physician and state legislator, periodically served in Congress between 1778 and 1787. DAB.

confusion, he endeavoured to turn the Attention to the house by an attack upon the secretary[4] who had contributed to the detection. In this he was also foiled. And he was obliged to sit still under the disgrace of having either lost his wit or his memory or of having no regard to truth.[5]

I am indeed heartily weary of this scene and if it continues much longer, I am inclined to think I shall wish to withdraw from it. Still however I entertain a fond hope that the same kind providence which has conducted us so far in our journey will open a way for the future happiness and prosperity of the United States. To his protection I recommend you and Am with sincere Affection, your loving husband

Cha Thomson

[4] Charles Thomson.

[5] The debate summarized here by Thomson was sparked by a July 11, 1783 memorial of the Massachusetts General Court that denounced Congress' commutation plan, which involved granting military officers full pay for five years instead of half-pay for life, as "inconsistent with that Equality which ought to subsist among Citizens of free and Republican States" and charged that the salaries of Congress' civil officers were inconsistent with "the State of our Finances, the Rules of Equity, and a proper regard for the public good." PCC, item 65, vol. II, fols. 185-88. In the end Congress adhered to its commutation plan but agreed to consider reductions in civil salaries. JCC, XXV, 571-87. For a fine analysis of the ideological dimensions of the struggle over half-pay and commutation, which are otherwise well described by Thomson, see Charles Royster, *A Revolutionary People at War: The Continental Army and American Character* (Chapel Hill, N.C., 1979), 333-51.

❖

Dear Hannah   Monday Octr. 13. 1783

Saturday was spent in fruitless debates about the temporary residence.[1] The unaccommodating spirit of some and the jealousy nay I may say the deep rooted hatred which others bear to the city of Philadelphia were displayed in the strongest colours. You will naturally ask to what cause can this be attributed. For my own part I am at a loss to determine. Much was said of the influence which that city had on the proceedings & acts of Congress. And yet this was disavowed by every man. Those who asserted it in the strongest terms were careful at the same time to intimate that it neither had nor could have any operation on them, and those that denied the influence, & some of them had long been members of & given the closest attendance to the business of Congress, declared they had never seen any symptoms of such influence. They considered the insinuation as dishonorable & called upon the assertors of this influence to produce a single instance of it. After repeated calls Mr. Gerry[2] undertook in a former day's debate to point out par-

RC (Princeton University Library: Charles Thomson Papers). Addressed: "Mrs. Thomson." Endorsed by Hannah Thomson: "1 week since at Princeton." This endorsement explains the long hiatus between this letter and the last one Thomson wrote to his wife on September 18, 1783.

[1] The issue of a permanent meeting place for Congress had already gone through several phases since the delegates first took up the question on October 6, 1783. In the first a coalition of delegates from New England and the Middle states combined on October 7 to designate a site by the Falls of the Delaware near Trenton as a permanent residence for Congress, a decision that offended the sectional sensibilities of southerners. Congress next considered where to meet while construction of the permanent seat was in progress and rejected in turn motions to adjourn to Philadelphia, Annapolis, and Williamsburg—the last on Saturday, October 11. Despite Congress' failure to agree on a temporary meeting place by the 13th, however, the votes on this issue clearly presaged the formation of a new coalition between New England and the South that was soon destined to succeed in winning congressional approval for a second permanent resident on the Potomac to complement the one planned for the Delaware. JCC, xxv, 654-60, 665-72.

[2] Elbridge Gerry (1744-1814), a graduate of Harvard College, 1762, whose name has enriched America's political lexicon, was a Massachusetts merchant and revolutionary leader who served two terms in Congress—1776-80 and 1783-85. George A. Billias, *Elbridge Gerry: Founding Father and Republican Statesman* (New York, 1976). As Thomson's letters reveal, Gerry was one of the principal architects of the emerging coalition between New England and the South mentioned in the previous note.

ticular instances. But those he produced were so contemptible, so ill grounded & baseless, as only to raise indignation and to shew that there was no foundation for the suspicion, that it was either imaginary or mere pretence. One of the instances he produced was in the conduct of Mr. Bingham[3] while he was agent in Martineque. A Boston Privateer had at an early period of the war & before France acknowledged the independence of America, captured a vessel in the west-Indies & carried his prize into Martineque. Complaint of this was made to the governor by the English, And as the governor wished to favour the Americans he evaded the complaint by ordering the vessel & cargo to be sold & the proceeds to [be] deposited in the hands of an Agent, till the matter could be enquired into. The Agent he fixed upon was Mr. Bingham, who appeared there only in the character of a merchant & who employed the proceeds for the public service in forwarding military stores for the use of our Army, at the same time informing Congress of his proceedings that they might take measures to reimburse him, if the Money should be ordered to be paid to the original owners or to satisfy the captors if it should be adjudged to them. After the treaty with France the captors instituted a suit against Bingham for the money. Bingham applied to Congress and Congress were so well satisfied with his conduct that they ordered the suit to be discontinued & took the matter upon themselves.[4] The other in-

[3] William Bingham (1752-1804), a graduate of the College of Philadelphia, 1768, was a wealthy merchant who served as Continental agent in Martinique from 1776 to 1780 and as a founder and director of the Bank of North America before representing Pennsylvania in Congress from 1786 to 1789. Robert C. Alberts, *The Golden Voyage: The Life and Times of William Bingham, 1752-1804* (Boston, 1969).

[4] The case of the *Pilgrim* and the *Hope* proved to be more complicated than Thomson realized. Early in 1779, the *Pilgrim*, a privateer owned by members of the powerful Cabot family of Massachusetts, captured the *Hope* "in the European seas" and brought her to Martinique, where Bingham examined her papers and decided that she was a neutral Danish merchantman not liable to seizure under the laws of privateering. Congress approved Bingham's decision and later the same year formally requested the Massachusetts General Court to persuade the Cabots to desist from a suit for damages they had brought against him. Unfortunately for Bingham, this request was made in vain. The Cabots subsequently produced convincing evidence that the *Hope* was a British ship using false papers, which meant that she was a lawful prize, and at length,

fluence was an affair which not long since happened near New Orleans. A privateer was fitted out at Boston to cruize off the mouth of the Mississippi. She there captured a ship that was not only under the protection of a flag, but under that of a spanish fort and in possession of a Spanish pilot sent out to conduct her in. There were sundry circumstances attending the capture, highly derogatory to the honor of the spanish flag and contrary to the laws of nations and these were aggravated by a flagrant breach of the laws of hospitality. The prize nevertheless being carried to Boston & libelled was condemned in the court of Admiralty, but on an appeal the judgment was reversed and thereupon Congress recommended it to the state of Massachusetts to take measures for punishing two of those concerned in the capture for the insult offered to the Spanish flag & the violation of the laws of neutrality. Though neither of the judges of the court of appeals who reversed the sentence were inhabitants of Pensylvania, yet this was quoted as an instance of the influence of Philada. on public measures.[5] On Saturday Mr. Lee[6] proceeded to quote the appointment of Mr. Morris & the powers vested in him as an instance of that influence. But though he did not convince any by this instance he confirmed the opinion that private pique & resentment were his governing principles. The motion that was under debate on Saturday was to remove to An-

---

after more than two decades of litigation, they finally collected $37,000 in damages from Bingham's estate shortly after his death in 1804. Alberts, *Golden Voyage*, 365-67, 430.

[5] For a comprehensive report by James Duane on the seizure of the Spanish merchant ship *St. Antonio* by the Massachusetts privateer *Polly*, see *JCC*, xxv, 546-48.

[6] Arthur Lee (1740-92), a member of the famous Lee family of Virginia, was a trained physician who received an M.D. from the University of Edinburgh in 1764 and a trained lawyer who pursued his legal studies at Lincoln's Inn and the Middle Temple in London. The highly contentious Lee was a prolific propagandist for the American cause in England for a number of years before the adoption of the Declaration of Independence, and thereafter he served for three tempestuous years as an American diplomatic commissioner to France in the course of which he became deeply involved in a bitter dispute with fellow commissioner Silas Deane that badly polarized Congress. After his recall from office in 1779, Lee returned to America and represented Virginia in Congress from 1781 to 1784. Louis W. Potts, *Arthur Lee: A Virtuous Revolutionary* (Baton Rouge, 1982).

napolis. Howell[7] declared that rather than go to Philadelphia, if the vote for Annapolis was lost, he would vote for Williamsburg or Charlestown nay even for Savannah in Georgia—That a Vote for Philadelphia was a high insult to the eastern states and this assertion passed uncontradicted by any member from those states, nay they seemed to confirm it by their unanimous vote to pass by Philadelphia & reside in Annapolis till next June. However the question was not carried. The debates were continued till after 4 P.M. and the house broke up in such very bad humour that I had some apprehensions they would not meet again. However upon recollection the members determined to continue in town, & try what can be done this morning. Yesterday I took a ride to Trenton to view the banks of the river. There is a delightful Spot on the Pensylvania side for a small town. It commands a very extensive & beautiful prospect both up & down the river & over the[8] Jersey & has many natural advantages; but the ground plot is rather too small. However I think it bids fair to be the place for the permanent residence of Congress and may hereafter be distinguished by the name of *Statesburg*. Adieu my dear Hannah. I hope you got safe home & found your family well. I am with sincere affection, your loving husband

Cha Thomson

[7] David Howell (1747-1824), a graduate of the College of New Jersey, 1766, who served as Professor of Mathematics and Natural Philosophy at Rhode Island College from 1769 to 1779 and then devoted himself to the legal profession, was a member of Congress for Rhode Island from 1782 to 1785. *Princetonians*, i, 562-67. In addition to being a zealous defender of state sovereignty in Congress, Howell was also one of the few delegates who regarded Princeton as a suitable meeting place for that body. See Burnett, *Letters*, vii, 279.

[8] Thus in ms.

--- ❖ ---

Dear Hannah,   Tuesday Oct 14 1783

I received your letter of the 12 by the Stage and was much pleased to hear of your safe arrival. You cannot be more uneasy than I am at our being separated. If the submitting to these inconveniences answered any good purpose, or if it were necessary for promoting the interest or happiness of our country I could more easily acquiesce. But I confess my situation is the more irksome as I plainly see that the measures which led to it and the spirit and temper which continue it evidently tend to a dissolution of the Union of these states and will if I am not greatly mistaken involve our country in new calamities. It cannot admit of a doubt that the peace, happiness and prosperity of these new and rising republics depend greatly on a close and intimate Union. And yet the temper, disposition and views of the inhabitants are so discordant, that I have serious apprehensions they will not be long kept together & that the predictions of our enemies will but too soon be verified in the dissolution of our Confederacy. Whether this is the intention of some men now in Congress or whether their conduct is guided by the prevailing sentiments of the states they represent or actuated by private motives I will not undertake to say. But this I will venture to assert particularly with regard to Howell, that were he in the pay of G. Britain I do not know any line of conduct he could pursue other than what he has done to answer his purpose and promote the designs of his employers. This you will say is harsh. It is so and I hope I may be mistaken. But the tenor of his conduct is so uniform, the means he uses to accomplish his purpose so unjustifiable and unrestrained by truth, and those purposes, in my opinion, so opposite to the interest, honor and dignity of the Union, that I cannot reconcile them with the true principles of policy and patriotism. I might say the same of some others who have co-operated with him; but they discover such strong traits of envy & personal resentment that these may in some degree account for their conduct.

Yesterday we had nine[1] states on the floor, and to day I am informed we may expect eleven. A motion was made by Mr. Mercer[2] and seconded by Mr. Lee to adjourn to Williamsburg. This I believe was made without any expectation of being carried. For an amendment, which was offered to shew that the adjournment was only for a temporary residence, was negatived by the mover and that being lost the eastern states could not give their assent & therefore the motion for Williamsburg was lost.[3] I am told it is in contemplation with some of the eastern states to propose a coalition with the southern and reconsider the vote for fixing the permanent residence near the falls of Delaware. And this being carried, either to fix the permanent residence at or near Georgetown on Potomack, or to establish two places for the meeting of Congress, one in or near the eastern states and the other in one of the southern states. This if carried will shew such a pointed resentment against Pensylvania and will so disoblige New Jersey, that I am confident it will throw them out of the Union. And the consequence will be that this Continent will be split into three divisions, the Eastern, middle & Southern. And all things considered I do not know but this may be for the general good & the best that can [be] done for the interest and happiness of the whole, provided the several districts confederate together for the purpose of general defence. It seems to be the order of providence that this world should be divided into a number of seperate & distinct governments.

Adieu my dear Hannah, take care of your health and rest assured of the unfeigned affection of your loving husband

Cha Thomson

RC (Princeton University Library: Charles Thomson Papers). Addressed: "Mrs. Thomson   Corner of Spruce & 4 Street   Philadelphia."

[1] Thomson first wrote "eight" and then changed it to "nine."

[2] John Francis Mercer (1759-1821), a Virginia lawyer who graduated from the College of William and Mary in 1775 and received legal training from Thomas Jefferson, rose to the rank of lieutenant colonel in the Continental Army during the War for Independence, served in Congress from 1782 to 1784, and then moved to Maryland where he held a variety of public offices. James Mercer Garnett, "John Francis Mercer, Governor of Maryland, 1801 to 1803," *Maryland Historical Magazine*, II (1907), 191-213.

[3] Mercer voted for his motion to adjourn Congress to Williamsburg, Va., "for the despatch of public business," but he opposed David Howell's amendment to replace these words with "for the place of their temporary residence." *JCC*, XXV, 675-76.

Dear Hannah   Wednesday Oct 15. 1783

It is mentioned by historians that the Emperor Titus recollecting that he had passed the preceding day without any act of benevolence or doing any worthy his high rank, broke out into this exclamation "O my friends I have lost a day." Those to whom the affairs of these infant states are entrusted, have little of the feelings or recollection of Titus or sure I am my ears might be frequently dinned with similar exclamations.

Yesterday Mr. Madison and Mr. Read returned from Philadelphia. It was expected that Mr. Rutledge[1] would have accompanied the latter. But as that was not the case and as Mr. Beresford did not attend and Delaware was unrepresented we had only nine states, so that the question about the temporary residence was not taken up. A report was therefore called for respecting Indian affairs and as this comprehended a paragraph relative to the expediency of laying off a district in the western country and erecting it into a seperate government as well for the purpose of satisfying the claims of the army as for the accommodation of such as might incline to become purchasers & settlers in that district, a question arose, in what manner they ought to be at first governed. It appeared evident at the first glance that it would be improper and dangerous to suffer people to settle that country without any restrictions or government. The land belonged to the United states, it was part of their territory & was to be disposed of for the benefit of the whole, & the people who should inhabit it when sufficiently numerous were to form a component part of the Union & to be entitled to a representation in the Congress of the United states. To set off a district and at once declare it to be a free, sovereign and independent state, would be to make a cession of it to the first

RC (Princeton University Library: Charles Thomson Papers). Addressed: "Mrs. Thomson   Philadelphia."

[1] John Rutledge (1739-1800), a South Carolina lawyer and future justice of the United States Supreme Court who studied at the Middle Temple in London, served as chief executive officer of South Carolina during the War for Independence and as a delegate to Congress from 1774 to 1775 and from 1782 to 1783. *DAB*.

stragglers who might settle there & would be a relinquishment of all the benefits expected to be derived from the sale of the lands; and to permit the first settlers to erect what government they pleased and under that government admit them into the Union might endanger the liberties of the confederated states & those republican principles which formed the basis of their several constitutions. For these reasons it was proposed that Congress should prescribe the terms of purchase & settlement, & prepare for them a temporary form of government, under which they should live till their numbers and circumstances were such as might intitle them to a representation in Congress, at which time they should be permitted to form a constitution for themselves not incompatible with the republican principles which are the basis of the other states in the Union. This was opposed by Rhodeisland out of a pretended zeal for liberty. Mr. Howell contended that the settlers whether few or many had a right immediately to form a constitution for themselves and to make laws for their own government; that denying them this privilege was to establish a tyranny. After a great deal of debate which consumed the day he was at last overruled by a vote and the house adjourned.[2] After the adjournment Mr. Fitzsimmons took leave of the members being determined as he said never [to] meet them again. I am really sorry Congress is deprived of his abilities. He is a man of great candour, sound judgment and well informed and was very useful especially in matters of accounts and finance.

I received no letter by yesterdays stage though I dare say you wrote. I hope you are well. Please to remember me to all friends.

I am with sincere affection, your loving husband

Cha Thomson

[2] See *jcc*, xxv, 678-79.

Dear Hannah   Thursday Oct 16. 1783

I have not received a line from you since that by the stage on Monday. I hope however you are well. Nothing is yet done with regard to the temporary residence and I begin to be afraid we shall be tied down for the winter to this uncomfortable village, notwithstanding eight states have resolved "that for the more convenient transaction of the business of the United states and accommodation of Congress it is expedient for them to adjourn from their present residence."[1] Yesterday for the first time since their removal from Philadelphia they seriously entered upon the business of the Continent and finished a very important matter relative to Indian Affairs.[2] But notwithstanding this I have little hopes of seeing the affairs of the Union in a happy train. You will see in the *Packet* of the 14th, under the Providence head, an extract of a letter from an American Minister dated Passy June 28 1783. The design of the Correspondent who furnished the extract is evidently to delude his constituents[3] and to induce a belief that our credit is high in Europe notwithstanding the noncompliance of the states with the five percent impost.[4] He knows in his conscience this is false. He

RC (Princeton University Library: Charles Thomson Papers). Addressed: "Mrs. Thomson   Philadelphia."

[1] Congress had approved this resolution on October 10, 1783 by a vote of seven states to three. *JCC*, xxv, 665.

[2] This day Congress adopted a report on Indian affairs that served as the basis for congressional Indian policy for the rest of the Confederation period. See *JCC*, xxv, 680-93; and Reginald Horsman, *Expansion and American Indian Policy, 1783-1812* (Michigan State University Press, 1967), ch. 1.

[3] Thomson first wrote "to delude the state" and then altered it to read as above.

[4] The September 27, 1783 issue of the *Providence Gazette* published an extract of a confidential letter from Benjamin Franklin and John Jay to the French foreign minister dated June 28, 1783. In this extract, which could only have been supplied by a member of Congress, the two American diplomats gave a glowing account of John Adams' success in negotiating a loan of five million guilders in the Netherlands. Thomson was convinced that David Howell had arranged for the publication of this item in order to undermine Congress' April 1783 request that the states authorize it to tax imported goods for twenty-five years so that it could liquidate the massive public debt accumulated during the recent conflict with Great Britain. Howell, who had played a leading role

had other letters from the ministers in his possession which shew that our credit is at a low ebb and that unless measures are speedily taken for establishing permanent funds for the regular payment of the interest and gradual discharge of the principal of the sums we have borrowed in Europe, it will quickly be totally annihilated & these rising states covered with infamy & disgrace if not involved in new & serious troubles. Had he meant to serve the true interest of his country he would have supplied his constituents with these extracts. But truth is not his object nor is it his wish to promote fœderal measures. What then are we to expect while such men are sent to represent a state in the Union?

Had this been the first instance of this correspondents disingenuity and disregard to truth, charity might lead one to think he was only mistaken, but when it is only a repetition of former mean tricks, when on another occasion he deceived his constituents with false information and desired to be furnished with extracts from a letter to gloss his lies, and a copy of the whole letter was delivered to him, instead of sending forward the letter which would have given a true state of facts he selected some detached scraps & sentences, sent them forward and left the letter on the table, it would be an insult on common sense to suppose him actuated by proper principles.[5]

I need not press you to write as often as you can and to inform

---

in bringing about the defeat of an earlier impost plan, feared that granting Congress the authority to tax—a power it was denied by the Articles of Confederation—would pose a serious threat to state sovereignty. For some indication of why Thomson held Howell responsible for the publication of the Franklin-Jay letter, see the following note.

[5] In December 1782 Congress had reprimanded David Howell for disclosing to a correspondent in Rhode Island without congressional authorization a confidential dispatch from John Adams dealing with his efforts to negotiate a loan in the Netherlands. In addition to violating his oath to preserve the confidentiality of congressional proceedings, this action also enfuriated nationalists in Congress because Howell took advantage of Adams' letter to argue that the prospect of receiving a substantial foreign loan obviated the need for Rhode Island to approve a request made by Congress in February 1781 for authority to levy an impost. See jcc, xxiii, 812-19, 821-22; and Burnett, Letters, vi, 509. The impost plans of 1781 and 1783 both failed to secure the unanimous approval of the states that was required to amend the Articles of Confederation.

me of what is passing in town, as you know how agreeable your letters are to, Dear Hannah, your affectionate Husband

Cha Thomson

Dear Hannah   Friday 17 Oct 1783.

The 17 of October is at length arrived, the day on which I hoped Congress would have returned. But I confess the prospect is as dark & gloomy as the morning is lowering. The underhand workings of the members seem in some manner to resemble the mountain in Germany mentioned in a late paper. Inward grumblings are heard; The head is covered with clouds & darkness. Vapours burst through apertures which destroy the trees and herbage and every thing denotes an approaching irruption which may involve the neighbourhood in one common ruin and calamity. I think I mentioned in a former letter that in order to engage the Southern States not to vote for a temporary residence in Philadelphia the eastern members had it in contemplation to propose two places for erecting buildings for the residence of Congress, one in the southern & one in the eastern or middle states. Mr. Gerry who has taken an active lead in this business, yesterday broached the matter and moved to have it considered but was prevented by a call for the Order of the day.[1] If the public treasury was full of money or if the public debts were paid, or funds provided for discharging them or even for the regular payment of the interest, one might hear such projects with patience. But in the present state of affairs to

RC (American Philosophical Society: Miscellaneous Manuscripts). Addressed: "Mrs. Thomson   Philadelphia."

[1] There is no mention of this "matter" in JCC under the date October 16, 1783. This day, however, Elbridge Gerry moved that in additon to the site by the Falls of the Delaware "buildings be likewise erected for the use of Congress, at or near the lower falls of Potomac or Georgetown." Congress decided to postpone consideration of Gerry's motion, which was seconded by Arthur Lee, until Wednesday, October 22, 1783, JCC, xxv, 697-99. This collaboration between a delegate from Massachusetts and one from Virginia symbolized the emergence of the coalition between New England and the South that was soon to carry the day in Congress on the capital site issue.

talk of building cities, when they can scarcely furnish money to buy paper on which to draw a plan of them, when they must be convinced that upon the Superintendant's quitting his office the few hopes that are kept together for the defence of west point and for guarding the public stores and magazines must disperse for want of provisions, the public creditors must go unpaid & the civil officers retire or serve the public at their own expense, Or in such a situation so pointedly to express their resentment against a city & state from which they have heretofore derived such assistance in money transactions appears to me something different from wisdom, prudence or policy. I am much mistaken if at this moment we are not puppets in the hands of the juggling politicians of Europe. Were I to hazard a conjecture it would be that G Britain in delaying the definitive treaty & restricting our commercial intercourse, has it in view to conclude the war by the provisional articles, to disunite us from France and by a future commercial treaty separate and apart to draw us into a close and intimate Union with Britain.[2] For this reason I do not expect any definitive treaty soon, other than a ratification of the provisional treaty. And I shrewdly suspect that G.B. will endeavour to weaken the bonds of Union between the states, by offers of different terms in trade and commerce to different states or parts of the Union. Divide and conquer was an old maxim with politicians. And in my Opinion it would be prudent in the states when they quit their arms not to forget the motto, *Join or die*, which was at the beginning of this contest displayed on so many of their colours.

I received your letter of Wednesday by yesterday's stage and am glad to find you in good health. I wish you could pay a particular attention to Mrs. Washington while in town. I find Mrs. Peters has

[2] Thomson's forebodings about British policy toward the new American nation were well grounded in the realities of the time. For well over a month he had been aware of the notorious Order in Council of July 2, 1783, which excluded American vessels from the vital British West Indian carrying trade, and of the publication of Lord Sheffield's celebrated *Observations on the Commerce of the American States* (London, 1783), a vigorous defense of the traditional mercantile system that provided the intellectual basis for Britain's highly restrictive postwar commercial relations with the United States. Congress had received an authentic text of the former enclosed with the diplomatic dispatches that arrived in Princeton on September 13, 1783, and at about the same time various American newspapers had begun to publish the latter.

invited her to dine. Could you not make a party & give her an invitation. I am glad you received my letters. They are written with freedom and I should be sorry any of them fell into improper hands.

Adieu my dear Hannah. Take care of your health. I am with sincere affection, your loving husband

Cha Thomson

Dear Hannah,   Sunday Oct 19. 1783

I have all your letters N. 1. 2. 3. & 4 now before me having again read them over with a view of answering them more particularly. But before I enter upon this, as I imagine you are anxious to know the result of yesterday, I must inform you that agreeably to the notice given a motion was made to reconsider the vote for postponing the Consideration of Mr. Gerry's motion till Wednesday next, and to take it up and decide upon it immediately. The situation of Mr. Van Berkel[1] & the necessity of giving him an Audience was held out as the ostensible reason, but the true one was that Mr. Izard was here on whose vote they could rely and he wanted to return to Philadelphia, and without his vote the measure could not be carried. It was in vain urged by the middle states that the measure was important & deserved serious deliberation, that the precipitancy with which it was about to be carried was unusual and unprecedented, that the moving without any just or solid reason to bring on a matter which the day before they had agreed to postpone for a few Days to give members time to deliberate was uncandid, especially as on the assurance & faith of that vote several members had gone out of town, particularly a member from Pen-

RC (Princeton University Library: Charles Thomson Papers).

[1] Pieter Johan van Berkel (1727-1800) served from 1783 to 1787 as the Netherlands' first ambassador to the United States. Jan Willem Schulte Nordholt, *The Dutch Republic and American Independence* (Chapel Hill, N.C., 1982), 252-54. Congress' reception of the Dutch ambassador at Princeton on October 31, 1783 is described in *JCC*, xxv, 780-86.

sylvania,[2] by whose absence his state was unrepresented; that such unsteady conduct would reflect dishonor on the public councils of America; That deciding the question on that day could not remove any difficulties out of the way or facilitate the means of receiving the Minister from Holland. If this Congress meant to receive him there were two ways to do it; one was to send for him to this place; the other was to go to a place at no great distance where they could receive him properly. The deciding or not deciding on the motion of the member from Massachusetts could have no effect upon the choice of either of these modes. If it was intended, upon carrying the vote for fixing another fœderal town on Potomack, to adjourn Congress to Annapolis, Members must be sensible that the distance of that place and the shortness of time would put it out of the power of this Congress to receive the Dutch minister. And when the Congress of the United states which is next to assemble will be able to receive him is very uncertain. The times of a great number of members expire with the present month. New Delegates are to be chosen, & some of the states are in such a situation that their legislatures cannot soon be convened. So that there is little prospect of a new Congress meeting for this or any other business till December. All these arguments passed unanswered, saving only that it was observed, that the presence or absence of Pensylvania was of no importance in the present case. The vote could & would be carried if it was present notwithstanding a negative;[3] that notice was given of the motion intended to be made for a reconsideration, the member for Pensylvania heard it and if he thought the vote of his state of importance he might have tarried; other gentlemen as well as he had business which required them to be absent and their tarrying here was very inconvenient. The question therefore was insisted on. When it was about to be put, the delegates for New Jersey in right of their state, agreeably to the rules of the house, required that the determination thereof should be put off till Monday next. And thus that matter now stands.[4] Congress yesterday

[2] Richard Peters. See Charles Thomson to Hannah Thomson, October 20, 1783.

[3] Thomson first wrote "their negative" and then altered it to read as above.

[4] James McHenry was the delegate who moved that Congress reconsider its decision to postpone consideration of Elbridge Gerry's motion for a second permanent residence on the Potomac until October 22, 1783. *jcc*, xxv, 702.

passed two proclamations, one for setting apart the second thursday in December next as a day of public thanks giving, and the other for disbanding all that part of the Army which had been furloughed,[5] so that there now remains in the service of the United states only those that are at West Point & the few at Philada. which by the bye have no business there, and I am astonished the state remains silent on that subject.

But I am wandering from my subject. You see, my dear, what it is to have a politician for a husband. Instead of love letters you are only to be entertained with business or politics. I confess my mind has been lately much agitated and I have deliberated very seriously on my future plan of life. My comfort and happiness greatly depends upon being with you. I have devoted so much of my life to, and spent so many anxious hours, or rather years, in the public service without emolument,[6] that I thought I might upon the return of peace and the attainment of those blessings for which we contended, continue to enjoy the profits arising from my Office, especially as the office is necessary and I flatter myself I should not be unserviceable to my country in the exercise of it. Nevertheless rather than be separated from you I would relinquish it, as I can now do it with honor and the cause of America will suffer no detriment, and I can do it with the less regret, as I am sensible that my continuance in Office will be constantly attended by envy though not with so much anxiety as I have heretofore experienced and that a small fault is sufficient to obliterate the Merit of many years faithful services. But I must premise that when I retire it will not be to ease and affluence. I must attend to some business for our support. However as our wants are not many and our expenses not very great, I think by attention to our farms we may live decently without much trouble or uneasiness of mind.

I have not had any answer about the purchase I made from Mr. Lawrence. I fancy they have taken the chance of the public sale.

---

[5] These proclamations, which were both drafted by James Duane, are in *JCC*, xxv, 699-701, 703-4.

[6] Thomson first wrote "much emolument" and then altered it to read as above. In fact he received total compensation in excess of $32,000 during his fifteen years of service as secretary of Congress. See Jennings B. Sanders, *Evolution of the Executive Departments of the Continental Congress, 1774-1789* (Chapel Hill, N.C., 1935), 180n.33.

If it there brings more, the answer I shall receive will be that the letter from Mr. Lawrence had miscarried or did not come in time & if less, then I may have it. Be it as it may, I am satisfied.

I think you had as well get the rooms papered. I do not think it can ever be done cheaper. The expense will be trifling. If you should have occasion for money make use of that received last. If Haddock calls for the price of the pipe, you will please to pay him and get him to put a cock into it near the pump to stop the water in the winter. I am sorry to give you trouble, but would be glad if you could have the wine racked off. Jonathan or Robert will at your desire get a cooper to do it.

Monday morning. I have nothing to add, but my most sincere wishes for your health and happiness and that I am with unfeigned affection, your loving husband

Cha Thomson

Dear Hannah,   Monday Evening Oct 20. 1783

As you must be anxious to know the result of this day's debate, I sit down to give you some account of it. The debates and proceedings beggar all description and the issue was fruitless. I informed you in my last that the question for reconsidering the vote which had postponed Mr. Gerry's motion to Wednesday was put off on Saturday by the state of New Jersey. It was therefore taken up this morning and all debates being precluded by the rules of the house, it was carried in the Affirmative by seven states. The vote for postponing to Wednesday which now came before the house was negatived, and the motion of Mr. Gerry was taken into Consideration.[1] Peters was gone to Philadelphia, Clarke[2] was con-

RC (Princeton University Library: Charles Thomson Papers).

[1] This day Congress voted along sectional lines to take up Elbridge Gerry's motion for a second permanent meeting place on the Potomac, with New England and the South in favor and the Middle states in opposition. *JCC*, XXV, 706-7.

[2] Abraham Clark (1726-94) was a New Jersey farmer, surveyor, and lawyer

fined to his bed by sickness & Condict[3] was absent. So that there were only eight states represented & of these there were three of the eastern and four of the southern, it was therefore expected that the motion for another fœderal town would be carried with ease and without much opposition. Mr. Montgomery who is inexperienced in the art of speaking, and has little command of the powers of Oratory had committed some thoughts to writing which he read and explained in a plain but very feeble manner. This offered an easy triumph to Mr. Gerry, who immediately rose to answer him. And though[4] he is far from being distinguished for his talents in Oratory, and cannot boast of the thunder of his voice, the harmony of his periods or any of those high strokes of eloquence which transport and captivate the hearers, nor of a just arrangement of arguments or soft insinuating address which commands the attention of an Audience and leads them insensibly and almost involuntarily to the point he means to carry, yet with his feeble voice and uncouth delivery broken and interrupted with many a heck & hem & repetition of ofs & ands he assumed such a superiority over Montgomery & treated his Arguments with such disdain as called up Duane, who enforced Montgomery's Argument & stated his own objections to the measure with great art, force and energy. But reasoning was lost and eloquence vain. The matter had been settled out of doors, and only waited the formality of a vote. The question was therefore called for. But just when it seemed ready to be put Mr. Howell got up and said he was not prepared to vote. He wanted first to have the temporary residence fixed. He was afraid after this vote was carried that Congress would be hurried away to Philadelphia; that it was to avoid this that he had agreed to give his vote for another fœderal town. He wished to be secured in this point, then he would be ready to give his vote. This objection at this stage of the business seemed to be quite unexpected

---

who served three terms in Congress—1776-78, 1780-83, and 1786-88. Ruth Bogin, *Abraham Clark and the Quest for Equality in the Revolutionary Era, 1774-1794* (East Brunswick, N.J. 1982).

[3] Silas Condict (1738-1801) was a New Jersey farmer and state legislator who served in Congress from 1781 to 1784. *Bio. Dir. Cong.*

[4] At this point Thomson first wrote and then deleted: "And though has little to boast of his talents."

and gave a new turn to the debates. It appeared evident that though the matter had been settled out of doors yet when it came to the point of decision they began to distrust each others sincerity and could not rely on each others candor. Their whole attention was therefore turned to the restoring mutual Confidence. For this purpose Mr. Carroll[5] proposed to tack a sentence to the motion, to empower & direct the president on a certain day to adjourn congress to meet at Annapolis there to sit for the dispatch of public business till the 31 of October following. This did not satisfy the eastern members as it threw the place of residence on Delaware wholly out of view. He therefore proposed to alter his motion to the 15 of October following & to add that on that day the president should be empowered & directed to adjourn congress to meet at Trenton the 31 of that month and that the sessions should be alternately 12 months at Annapolis & 12 months at Trenton till the buildings were erected in the two fœderal towns & fit for the reception of Congress. The term of 12 months did not please Ellery, he wanted it to be confined to 6 and declared he could not give his assent without that alteration. On the other hand Mr. Izard declared that he would not agree to a shorter term than 12 months and as the assent of both was necessary Carroll who was deeply interested in the vote withdrew his motion & said he would trouble himself no farther in the matter. He appeared to be extremely mortified. Gerry then undertook to draw up a conciliating motion & for this purpose proposed that the residence should be alternately at equal periods of not more than one year nor less than six months in Trenton & Annapolis until the buildings to be erected on the banks of the Delaware and Potomack should be prepared for the reception of Congress. Upon this Ellery moved to strike out the words "one year nor less than" so as to confine the residence to a term of not more than 6 mo. And as by the rules of the house the question must be stated "shall the words stand," and the votes of seven states were necessary to keep them in, his single negative was sufficient to remove them. However for the sake of conciliation

[5] Daniel Carroll (1730-96), the brother of Bishop John Carroll, was a Maryland merchant and landholder who owned several tracts of land in the vicinity of the proposed Potomac meeting site and served in Congress from 1782 to 1783. *DAB.*

his collegue[6] & the state of Massachusetts joined him in the vote and the words were struck out. Upon this a motion was made to strike out the remaining words "of not more than 6 months" and reduce Gerry's conciliatory motion to the simple proposition of residing alternately at equal periods in Trenton & Annapolis, which was accordingly done; but in that state it did not meet the approbation of Ellery & for want of his vote it was lost.[7] Howell was now reduced to his former difficulty & declared he could not give his consent to the Original motion. This threw all into confusion, from debate and argument they proceeded to reproaches & altercation. The middle states not less pleased than surprized at this sudden and unexpected turn stood by silent spectators and enjoyed the confusion. As it was now near sunset & Mercer who was agitated in a high degree was proceeding to lay open the whole scene of this secret transaction with some severe reflections on the disingenuity and want of candour in the eastern members, and as all hopes of an accommodation were now at an End, an adjournment was called for which put an end to further dispute & thus for the present the project of another fœderal town is vanished in air. The fall of the south sea stocks hardly gave a greater shock to the proprietors than the bursting of this bubble to its projectors. The southern members now declare that they will vote for the temporary residence at Philada. But I question whether they will adhere to this when they cool. I am rather inclined to think matters will rest as they are till the new Congress meets.

Adieu my dear Hannah, take care of your health & remember me to all friends. I am with sincere affection, your loving husband

Cha Thomson

Molly comes to invite [me] to breakfast & desires me always to send her love to you.

Tuesday morning Oct 21. 1783

P.S. Notwithstanding the defeat of yesterday I understand the eastern and So. States are rallying their forces & mean this morning to bring on the subject again & for that purpose Mr. Izard is de-

---

[6] David Howell.

[7] For the various motions and votes on a temporary seat for Congress described by Thomson in this letter, see *JCC*, xxv, 707-10.

tained in town. I fancy some new convention is entered into. There is no possibility of conjecturing with any degree of certainty what may be the event. The jarring atoms may for a time be combined, even grains of sand will by being wet for awhile adhere, but the cohesion will not be lasting.

C.T.

Dear Hannah,   Tuesday Evening Oct 21. 1783

The dye is cast. The vote is taken and carried for a second fœderal town and for the removal of Congress to Annapolis. Time must determine the wisdom or impolicy of the measure. For my own part to use an expression of lord Botetourt[1] I augur no good of it. Agreeably to what I mentioned in my postscript of this morning, the eastern delegates after Congress broke up yesterday got together and came to an agreement, upon which Mr. Izard was detained in town, And this morning as soon as the journals & dispatches were read, the motion of Mr. Gerry was revived. Whereupon Ellery got up and informed the house, that he found himself disposed to accommodate and with that view would move an Amendment, which was accordingly made & seconded and quickly passed.[2] It was in vain to oppose, the measure was determined on and argument was useless: The opposing members therefore contented themselves with silent votes in the negative. There were only eight states present, and as soon as the vote was carried Mr. Izard withdrew & seven only were left, a number inadequate by the articles

RC (Princeton University Library: Charles Thomson Papers). Addressed: "Mrs. Thomson   Philadelphia."

[1] Norbonne Berkeley, Baron de Boutetourt, was royal governor of Virginia from 1768 to 1770.

[2] William Ellery's motion, which was approved by the now familiar coalition of delegates from New England and the South, provided that "until the buildings to be erected on the banks of the Delaware and Potomac shall be prepared for the reception of Congress, their residence shall be alternately at equal periods of not more than one year, and not less than six months in Trenton and Annapolis." *JCC*, xxv, 711-12.

of confederation to any great national purposes. And much I fear the number will not soon be augmented. The jarring interests of the states appear almost in every question.

The Indian nations with whom we have lately been at war having signified their desire of peace, instructions were drawn up for the direction of those who should meet & confer[3] with them.[4] There are several gentlemen who were appointed Commissioners for Indian affairs in 1775 and who have ever since held all the conferences and managed all business with the Indians. Among these commissioners are genl. Schuyler and Mr. Douy of the state of New York.[5] These gentlemen being Newyorkers are obnoxious to the Eastern states. It was therefore proposed to elect new commissioners for managing the ensuing treaty. And Mr. Gerry who seems to be used as the instrument for setting this continent in a flame, among other arguments mentioned the necessity and propriety of Massachusetts having men in the commission in whom she could confide as she claimed all the lands to the westward, the whole breadth of her state across New York and to the utmost extent of the boundary of the United states; and that he was under instructions to support that claim & to oppose every measure in Congress that had the least tendency to invalidate it.[6] This you may well imagine alarmed the delegates of New York. Mr. Duane replied with warmth and some acrimony. It was very strange he said if Massachusetts had such a claim to the lands in the state of New York that she should suffer it to be so long dormant. That the state of New York had been in the possession of the lands now claimed for more than 150 years. Why was it not brought forward and settled agreeably to the articles of Confederation while common danger kept the states united. Was it reserved to this time that after New York had wasted her best blood and treasure and debilitated herself by her exertions in the common cause advantage might be taken of her weakness

[3] Thomson first wrote "should hold treaty" and then altered it to read as above.

[4] See Charles Thomson to Hannah Thomson, October 16, 1783, note 2.

[5] Gen. Philip Schuyler and Volkert Douw were the Indian commissioners in question.

[6] The historical background of the boundary dispute between Massachusetts and New York, which was not finally resolved until 1787, is described in Philip J. Schwarz, *The Jarring Interests: New York's Boundary Makers, 1664-1776* (Albany, N.Y., 1979), chs. 5-7, 12-13.

and the longest sword decide the controversy? He remarked on the ungenerous treatment New York had received from the eastern states in the affair of Vermont.[7] That while she was surrounded with enemies and exerting her whole force to repel common danger they were laying schemes to raise up enemies in her bowels and to enrich themselves with her spoil. Rhodeisland thought she should have a commissioner to manage her interests at the ensuing treaty as she had a right to a share of the western country. Maryland also put in her claim. In short the whole scene was an illustration of the fable of the hunters quarreling about the bear skin, before they had killed the bear. It was at last proposed that two commissioners should be chosen from each state. This was to me another strong symptom[8] of the approaching dissolution of the Union. Nothing however was decided. I suppose it will be a subject of debate to-morrow.

I must now think seriously of my future plan of life. I want to consult & advise with you. But am afraid I shall not be able to go down before the dissolution of this wise Congress. Mr. Bond informs me he intends to quit the Office on friday. I would have you nevertheless proceed to have the rooms & entry papered and should be glad you would speak to Griffits to fit up a place for our carriage.—By this you will perceive I have received your letter of Sunday. Enclosed I send you a copy of the resolution passed today. I wish I could say I had even the smallest or most distant prospect of the salutary effects held forth in the preamble. I confess I have not the least. However we have seen great events and we have experienced an unseen hand guiding us to them. All may terminate well.

"The ways of providence are dark and intricate

[7] Under the terms of the charter the Duke of York received from his royal brother in 1664, New York claimed jurisdiction over Vermont, which had proclaimed herself an independent republic in 1777. New York's relinquishment of this claim in 1790 brought the controversy to an end and paved the way for Vermont's admission to the union in the following year. Duane's defense of New York's jurisdictional rights was scarcely the act of a disinterested public servant, for he laid claim to several large tracts of land in Vermont on the basis of grants from the government of New York that were not recognized as valid by the Green Mountain state.

[8] Thomson first wrote "the strongest symptom I have yet seen" and then altered it to read as above.

"Puzled in mazes and perplexed in errors
"Our understanding traces them in vain"[9]
Let me therefore conclude with the pious poet
"Je crains mon Dieu, que j'aye ne point d'autre crain."[10]
Adieu my dear Hannah, take care of your health. I am
with sincere affection, your loving husband

Cha Thomson

ENCLOSURE

By the United States in Congress assembled
Tuesday Oct 21 1783

Whereas there is reason to expect that the providing buildings
for the alternate residence of Congress in two places will be pro-
ductive of the most salutary effects by securing the mutual confidence and affections of the states, it is therefore Resolved that
buildings be likewise erected for the use of Congress at or near the
lower falls of Potomack or Georgetown, provided a suitable district
on the banks of the river can be procured for a fœderal town and
the right of soil and an exclusive jurisdiction or such other as
Congress may direct shall be vested in the United states; and that
until the buildings to be erected on the banks of the Delaware and
Potomack shall be prepared for the reception of Congress, their
residence shall be alternately at equal periods of not more than
one year and not less than six months in Trenton and Annapolis,
and the president is hereby authorised and directed to adjourn
Congress on the 12 day of November next to meet at Annapolis
on the 26 day of the same month for the dispatch of public business.

[9] These lines are spoken by Portius in Joseph Addison's *Cato* (1713), 1.1.48-
50, a play whose stirring defense of liberty made it a great favorite among
colonial Americans. It is interesting to note that Addison used the word "heaven"
rather than "providence."
[10] "I fear God and have no other fear." This is a fairly faithful paraphrase
of the words spoken by Joad in Jean Racine's *Athalie* (1691), 1.1.64: "Je crains
Dieu, cher Abner, et n'ai point d'autre crainte."

Dear Hannah,   Thursday Oct 23. 1783

Yesterday the gentlemen from Pensylvania attended & with them Madison & Bland in expectation the question for a second fœderal town would be brought on. Judge what their surprize must have been when they found it decided. But as if what was done would not sufficiently irritate Pensylvania the states of Massachusetts & Rhodeisland seem determined to drive her to desperation. The legislature of Pensylvania at their last session judging it proper and necessary, in order to satisfy the promises made to their officers & men to purchase of the Indians their claim to the lands within the boundary of the state, applied to Congress for leave to send commissioners to the proposed treaty to make the purchase. This was referred to a comee. who highly approved the application of the legislature, pointed out the wisdom & good policy of the step, & recommended that the commissioners should give notice to the executive of Pensylvania of the time & place of holding the treaty in order that the commissioners of the state might attend, and that the commisioners of the United states should be instructed to give them every aid but so as not to be incompatible with the interests of the United states & the purposes they had in view. This was opposed by the delegates of Massachusetts & Rhodeisland, under pretence that it was contrary to the Articles of Confederation, that it might enhance the demands of the Indians for the land which the United states wanted to purchase or give an advantage to Pensylva. in making her purchase. Mr. Gerry seemed to intimate that he would agree to the measure, if Pensylvania would throw what she meant to give to the Indians into a common stock with the United states, & the commissioners for the United states had the sole management of the business. But this being refused, Massachusetts & Rhodeisland voted against the report and the application was rejected, there being only six of the eight states present in favour of the measure.[1] Fain would I hope that Pensylvania by her

RC (Princeton University Library: Charles Thomson Papers). Addressed: "Mrs. Thomson   Philadelphia."

[1] See *JCC*, xxv, 717-19.

wisdom and magnanimity would shew herself superior to these insults & will not suffer herself to be driven into any intemperate measures. Sure I am that if she can for a short time persevere in the temperate conduct she has lately pursued she will in spite of the malice of her enemies establish her character for wisdom & moderation not only among the United states but among all the nations of Europe. The measures lately pursued by Congress will in a very short time reduce the United states to great distress & difficulties. I am much mistaken if the steps already taken will not ruin the measures of the Superintendt. so that by the 12th. of next month, the time they have directed the president to adjourn Congress to Annapolis, the United states in Congress assembled will not be able to command as much money as will pay for removing their papers. Little do our shortsighted politicians dream of the precipice upon which they are standing or into what distress they are plunging their country. Their minds are intoxicated with their late success and their judgment blinded by passion and prejudice. Distress and dishonor will awaken people to their senses. The causes of it will be known and I shall not be surprized if those who have led them into it quickly feel the effects of their resentment.

I received your letter of tuesday. I beg you would not suffer your mind to be too much disturbed. Things will not long remain in their present situation. Either good sense & moderation will quickly reassume their place in our national council & we shall yet see happy days or the fabrick of our government will soon be destroyed & you and I, like doves to their windows, will retire to the enjoyment of our private estate.

Adieu my dear Hannah, take care of your health and keep up your spirits, & rest assured in all occurrences of the unfeigned affection, with which, I am, your loving husband

Cha Thomson

Dear Hannah   Friday Oct 24. 1783

I spent a pretty curious day yesterday and will endeavour to give an account of some of the incidents. In the morning I went rather earlier than usual to the office as I wanted to compleat a piece of business. Soon after Messrs. Howell and Tilton[1] came in. Mr. Howell said if I was not too busy they would wish to speak to me. I desired to know their pleasure. They said they wanted to consult me on an application from Mr. Gordon, who was preparing to write a history of the revolution & wished to be allowed Access to the offices & to be admitted to examine all the secret papers and transactions of Congress.[2] That I told him was a matter of which they were best able to judge. They wanted my Opinion. I told them if I were to hazard an Opinion it would be that the time and circumstances of our affairs would not admit of it. The design of Mr. Gordon as an historian was to develope the secret springs & motives of Action, to trace and scan the conduct of the persons engaged in public councils & public measures, to find out if possible by what motives they were guided, whether in the determination of votes of importance & in their general conduct they were actuated & guided by the public good, by state politics or by passion, resentment or private interest. In short to enter into their hearts & thoughts, & delineate them to the world in their true Characters. And no doubt he expected & possibly might find, in rumaging the papers in the secretary['s] Office, some original reports, motions

RC (Princeton University Library: Charles Thomson Papers).

[1] James Tilton (1745-1822), a Delaware physician who received A.B. and M.D. degrees from the College of Philadelphia in 1768 and 1771, served as a regimental surgeon in the Continental Army during the War for Independence and as a delegate to Congress from 1783 to 1785. DAB.

[2] Curiously enough there is no mention in the official records of Congress of the Rev. William Gordon's "application" or of the appointment of a committee to consider it. In response to a later application from the English-born clergyman and historian, however, Congress agreed on May 25, 1784 to grant Gordon access to all of its records save those "which hitherto have been considered confidential or secret." JCC, xxvii, 427-28. Gordon's history of the American Revolution was subsequently published under the title *The History of the Rise, Progress and Establishment of the United States of America*, 4 vols. (London, 1788).

or minutes that might lead to this knowledge. Again from the Office for foreign affairs he doubtless expected a clue to lead him to the characters of our ministers abroad, to trace the causes of their disputes and differences, which had done us no honour in the eyes of foreign nations; to find out the opinions they had formed of foreign courts, the advice they had given, the instructions under which they had acted, & the ends and objects which Congress had in view and the means they had used to attain them. In order that he might from thence embellish his history with reflections useful to posterity. In like manner I might proceed to the war department & office of finance. But from what I had said I submitted to their judgment, whether the present situation of our affairs & the present time would admit such an investigation. For my own part I feared it would not. Besides the present unsettled state of Congress, and the deranged state of the offices was a farther objection. Mr. Howell said he was very much of my opinion & was obliged to me for it. The application of Mr. Gordon was referred to them, & they wanted to know my opinion before they reported.[3]

In the afternoon I dined at the presidents. Before dinner Howell attached himself to me and seemed uncommonly complaisant. In the morning the military establishment in time of peace had been under debate, and the power of Congress to garrison any posts or keep up any troops in time of peace was a subject of discussion in which he and his collegue Ellery had taken a warm part, and which they opposed with great vehemence, insisting that by the articles

[3] Thomson eventually concluded that an objective history of the American Revolution revealing the true motives of its participants would be contrary to the best interests of the new American nation. "I ought not," he explained in declining one of many requests that he himself take advantage of his unparalleled knowledge and experience to write such a history, "for I should contradict all the histories of the great events of the Revolution, and shew by my account of men, motives, and measures, that we are wholly indebted to the agency of providence for its successful issue. Let the world admire the supposed wisdom and valor of our great men. Perhaps they may adopt the qualities that have been ascribed to them, and thus good may be done. I shall not undeceive future generations." George W. Corner, ed., *The Autobiography of Benjamin Rush* (Princeton, 1948), 155. Thus, adhering to the ancient exemplar tradition of historiography, Thomson came to believe that preserving an accurate record of the events of the Revolution was less important than nurturing the spirit of American nationalism by fostering a mythological view of the Revolution's heroes.

of Confederation the United states in Congress assembled had no right or power to garrison a single fort or keep up a single soldier in time of peace. That it rested with every individual state to provide for its own security and defence, and that Congress had only the right to judge of the quantum or degree of force which each should keep up and that the general defence was provided for by that part of the articles which enjoined on each state to keep up a well regulated militia. That if a power was admitted to be in Congress to garrison posts & keep up troops it would be necessary to have it defined, least it should be abused to the injury of the individual states &c.

On this subject he asked my Opinion. I told him that in matters of peace and war and what related to the general defence and common welfare the sovereign power of the United states was vested in Congress. That in every Sovereign there was a latent power to provide for the common safety and defence. To deny the existence of this power would be absurd, to delineate & define it strictly would be dangerous. While it was employed for the public good & general safety no one could complain. If ever it was abused, it would be easy for the states to repress and restrain it. But considering the constitution of Congress, there was little danger of such an abuse. I therefore thought that in the present question a discussion of the power of Congress was unnecessary and that the only enquiry ought to be whether the public safety required the garrisoning of some posts, what posts those ought to be and what force will be necessary to maintain them. This being agreed on, it will then be necessary to consider on what footing they are to be established & how they are to be raised & kept up. He was pleased to say there was weight in what I said.[4] At dinner I happened to

[4] This exchange of views between Thomson and David Howell brilliantly illuminates the differences that existed at the time over the issue of the military policy America should pursue after the conclusion of peace with Great Britain. On one side a group of Continental Army officers and nationalist leaders in Congress, convinced that the country required a strong defense establishment to safeguard the coasts and the western frontier, advocated the creation of a standing army of professional soldiers backed by an elaborate system of arsenals, magazines, fortifications, and military schools and supplemented by a thoroughly reorganized state militia system under national control. In contrast localist leaders, suspicious of standing armies, eager to preserve state sovereignty, and aware that the Articles of Confederation gave Congress no authority

be seated between him and Mr. Gerry. I could not help smiling at my situation. The Minister of France had arrived in town and was at the table. At dinner the president who loves to talk and is not very curious in his choice of subjects started a conversation about the propriety of selling instead of removing the furniture of the president's house. Mr. Peters observed that the expence of removing furniture backwards & forwards must be great, that selling it at every removal would incur a considerable loss. That therefore it would be necessary to have two setts, & instead of selling the furniture now he submitted whether it would not be best to keep it here till Congress returned & applying to Mr. Gerry asked whether this was not good eastern economy. I observed to my Assessors that I fancied it would be necessary to sell the furniture to raise money to defray the expense of removing the papers. This led Mr. Howell to our finances & consequently to Mr. Morris. He had a great respect for Mr. Morris and his state were perfectly sensible of the great services he had done to the United states, but they were opposed to his plans and measures. That for his own part all his opposition arose from that and whatever might be thought, it never was his intention to injure him in his private capacity or character. I told him it was not for me to enter into any gentleman's thoughts or intentions. I could only judge of actions. However I would put several circumstances together and leave others to form a conclusion. Mr. Morris had entered into his Office at a time when there was an end of all public credit, when our army was on the point of disbanding for want not of pay but of provisions, when those who were enemies to our cause were pluming themselves with

----

to raise military or naval forces in peacetime, opposed plans for an elaborate peacetime military establishment and preferred instead to rely on the state militia as the nation's primary means of defense. Thomson and Howell discussed these issues at this time because Congress was then considering a report on the peacetime military establishment drafted by Alexander Hamilton that embodied most of the leading nationalist views on this issue. Congress largely ignored Hamilton's recommendations, but in the end the imperatives of frontier defense induced the delegates in 1784 to organize a small hybrid force of men drawn from certain state militias that stood somewhere between a traditional standing army and a regular militia unit. See Richard H. Kohn, *Eagle and Sword: The Federalists and the Creation of the Military Establishment in America, 1783-1802* (New York, 1975), chs. 3-4.

hopes of our speedy ruin, the timid & wavering seemed ready to provide for their safety by going over to the enemy & the most stout hearted had the most serious apprehensions of distress & danger. Without a farthing in the public treasury, without any well grounded hopes of a speedy supply, Mr. M stept into office & by his personal credit & wise measures retrieved & established credit & fed & kept the army together, until the enemy were compelled to acknowledge our independence and agree to a cessation of hostilities. When after this he was desirous of quitting the office, he was induced to continue till the army was disbanded. This he agreed to on Condition that an application should be made to the court of france for a farther aid of money and an earnest recommendation sent to the states to forward the supplies called for and on a most solemn assurance given by Congress to aid & support him in the measures he should take. On these conditions & assurances he continued And proceeded to issue his notes & enter into engagements until his anticipations amounted to a million of dollars. The moment this was known he, Mr H, had heard a motion to countermand the application to the court of France, to suspend the payment or collection of the taxes called for, and enquiries made by what authority Mr. M. issued notes & intimations thrown out that he was liable in his private capacity to be sued for those notes by the holders. Put all these together & what judgment is to be formed. He drew his face into a smile, which he has always at command & said aye, indeed, put all these together and it looks bad.

In the mean while Peters had darted some strokes of wit at Gerry which seemed to touch him and as he has a great inclination to be thought a wit though I hardly ever knew any who had less pretensions to it he turned to me and said he had told somebody, I do not recollect whom he named, that he must do one of two things though he believed he would chuse the last, either to stay in Congress and learn to be a Salamander & live in fire, or to leave Congress. I told him if Gentlemen continued in the disposition they had lately discovered it would be proper to learn the use of the sword and to come armed to Debate. That if they acted and spoke conformable to the general sentiments of their constituents it was no matter how soon they parted. The sooner the better. For jarring interests prosecuted with such temper could never coalesce. And if they seperated before enmity took deep root, by mutual reproaches their common safety and common danger might the sooner bring the states together on better terms.

I concluded the evening with the perusal of a pamphlet, sent me by Mr. Dunlap,[5] on a quarrel that has taken place in France between Mr. Laurens & one Edmund Jennings,[6] a gentleman from Maryland.[7]

The enclosed note from Mr. Lawrence will inform you of the state of affairs between him & me.

I am, my dear Hannah, your loving husband

Cha Thomson

Dear Hannah   Saturday Oct 25. 1783

I received yours of thursday N. 7, And was exceedingly surprized and much concerned to find upon opening it that you had not received a letter from me since Sunday. I had written with great freedom and sent a letter every day by the stage directing it to be given to the driver and not to any of the passengers, that you might receive it the same evening. I was somewhat relieved by the postscript, which informed that mine of Monday & Tuesday had got

[5] John Dunlap (1747-1812) was the celebrated Philadelphia printer who published the first broadside of the Declaration of Independence.

[6] Thomson first wrote "& I forgot the man" and then altered it to read as above.

[7] Henry Laurens, an American peace commissioner in Paris who had once served as president of Congress, and Edmund Jenings, a shadowy figure who was suspected by many of his contemporaries of being a British secret agent, were involved in a bitter dispute over Laurens' charge that Jenings had deliberately fomented dissension among the American peace commissioners in order to serve the interests of Great Britain—an accusation Jenings vigorously denied. This controversy prompted both men to write pamphlets defending their positions of which Jenings' *The Candor of Henry Laurens, Esq; Manifested by His Behaviour to Mr. Jenings* (London, 1783) is undoubtedly the one mentioned by Thomson. Jenings' behavior during the American Revolution was so equivocal that historians are still unable to decide whether he was in fact a British spy. See "The Affair of the Anonymous Letters" in James H. Hutson, ed., *Letters from a Distinguished American: Twelve Essays by John Adams on American Foreign Policy, 1780* (Washington, D.C., 1978), 51-66.

Chevalier de La Luzerne by Charles Willson Peale
Oil on canvas
Courtesy of Independence National Historical Park Collection

to hand. I wish you would direct Peter to attend every evening at the Indian King till the stage comes in and to search the box & pocket of the stage where the letters are kept. You may depend that one goes by every stage. And I should be sorry any were lost. It would make me more cautious in expressing my sentiments.

I am much pleased with the attention you paid to Mr. Spear & his daughter. We are under obligations to him, which I longed to repay. You have not told me what sort of a girl his daughter is, nor given me any account of our Baltimore friends.

As I mean the carriage house only for a temporary convenience I would have it made of rough boards and am very indifferent where it is placed. I think it may as well be placed on the street adjoining the enclosed lot. It will serve for a lime house if ever I should build.

I will not trouble you with any anxiety about my future plan of life. I can form none for happiness or satisfaction in this world, unless you are with me. I am now advanced in life and find myself much more helpless for having been so long helped and tended by you. And yet I confess I have a strong desire, to watch the workings of the present ferment, to mark the characters of the present actors and to see the issue of present measures. The Minister of France[1] made a remarkable Observation, the evening before last at the President's. "I told col. Hamilton," said he, "he was putting the Chesnuts in the fire to roast, but another might eat them. I fancy he now finds I was a true prophet." I leave you to judge what opinion he has of the late removal.[2]

Adieu my dear Hannah, take care of your health. I am with sincere affection, your loving husband

Chas Thomson

RC (Princeton University Library: Charles Thomson Papers). Addressed: "Mrs. Thomson   Philadelphia."

[1] Chevalier de La Luzerne, on whom see Charles Thomson to Hannah Thomson, June 30, 1783, note 1.

[2] In view of Thomson's evident distaste for Alexander Hamilton it seems ironic to note that when Thomson encountered difficulties in securing payment of his salary arrears from the new federal government in 1789 it was Secretary of the Treasury Hamilton who intervened and ensured that Thomson received all the money due him. See Burnett, *Letters*, VIII, 835-36; and Harold C. Syrett et al., eds., *The Papers of Alexander Hamilton*, 26 vols. (New York, 1961-79), V, 381.

INDEX

❖

Continental Army (*cont.*)
of, 76; half-pay for officers of,
58-61; land for, 54; mutiny in
Philadelphia, xl-xliv, 6, 8-9, 12,
25-26
Continental Congress: accepts Virginia's land cession, 52-54; addresses to, 19, 22, 25, 27-29, 32-
34, 44, 57, 59-61; alleged meeting at Prospect, 5; attendance
in, 7, 18, 20, 25, 27, 28, 32, 37,
51, 67, 68, 75, 78; audience with
Washington, 45; and case of *St.
Antonio*, 64; celebrates Independence Day, 16; commissions
bust of Washington, 48-49;
compensates disabled seamen,
55; considers Marine Department, 56-57; debates half-pay,
58-61; historical sketch of, xxv-
xlv; and Indian policy, 68, 70,
82-83, 85, 86; meeting place for,
10-12, 19, 29, 32, 37, 39-41, 44,
46, 49-51, 54-55, 62-65, 67, 70,
72-73, 74-75, 77-84; meets in
Nassau Hall, 5-6; moves to
Princeton, xliv, 8-9; need for
funds, 72-73; and peacetime
military establishment, 88-90;
and Philadelphia mutiny, xl-xliv,
12; proclamations of, 75-76;
proposed adjournment to Philadelphia, 39-41, 52, 53, 62, 80;
and public debt, 46, 54; ratifies
peace treaty, 24; ratifies treaty
with Sweden, 37; receives foreign dispatches, 51; reprimands
David Howell, 70-71; return to
Philadelphia sought, 6, 9-10, 14,
22, 25-26, 27-29, 32-34, 46; and
suit against William Bingham,
63; and territorial government,
68-69; voting in, xxvii-xxviii, 18
Continental Court of Appeals, 64
Continental Navy, 55, 57
Cornwallis, Charles, Lord, xxxii,

xxxviii-xxxix, 56
Dayton, Elias, 44
Deane, Silas, xx, xxviii, xxix, xxx,
xxxi, 64
De Grasse, François Joseph Paul,
Comte, xxxix
Delaware, xxvii, xxxiii, 30, 51, 68
Delaware, Falls of: as meeting
place for Congress, 62, 67, 72,
79, 81, 84
Dickinson, John, xiv, xvi, xxix,
xxx, xxxi, xl, xlii, xliv, xlv, 6, 9,
10, 26, 27, 31
Dickinson, Mary Norris (Mrs.
John Dickinson), 31
Douw (Douy), Volkert, 82
Duane, James, 26, 29, 32, 33, 45,
64, 76, 78, 82, 83
Duffield, George, 22
Dunlap, John, 92
Dupre, Augustin, 56
Du Simitière, Pierre Eugène, 21

Elizabethtown, N.J.: address to
Congress, 44
Ellery, William, 7, 12, 55, 60, 79,
80, 81, 88
Ellsworth, Oliver, xxxv
*An Enquiry into the Causes of the Al-
ienation of the Delaware and Sha-
wanese from the British Interest*
(Charles Thomson), xiii

FitzSimons, Thomas, 17, 27, 49,
52, 69
France, 63, 73; application to for
loan to U.S., 91
Franklin, Benjamin, xii, xiii, xv,
xxviii, xxix, xxx, xxxi, xxxvi, 37,
56, 70
*Freeman's Journal; or, The North
American Intelligencer*, 18
Friendly Association, xiii
Friends Public School, xii, xiii

Galloway, Joseph, 47

Gates, Horatio, xxxvi
Georgetown, Md.: as meeting
  place for Congress, 67, 72, 84
Georgia, xxvii, 54; delegates to
  Congress, 18
Germantown, Pa.: address to Con-
  gress, 49-51
Gerry, Elbridge, 62, 63, 72, 74,
  75, 77, 78, 79, 80, 81, 82, 85,
  90, 91
Gibelin, E. A., 56
Gordon, William, 87-88
Great Britain: commercial policy
  toward U.S., 73; peace treaty
  with, 24, 54, 73
Green, Ashbel, 16
Greene, Nathanael, xl
Griffiths (Griffits), Mr., 83

Haddock, Mr., 77
Hamilton, Alexander, xlv, 3, 8-10,
  17, 32, 37, 40, 90, 94
Harriton (Charles Thomson's es-
  tate), xxi
Hawkins, Benjamin, xlii, xliv
Henry, Patrick, xxxvi
Higginson, Stephen, 55
*The History of the Rise, Progress and
  Establishment of the United States
  of America* (William Gordon), 87
Holten, Samuel, 60
*The Holy Bible, Containing the Old
  and New Covenant, Commonly
  Called the Old and the New Testa-
  ment* (Charles Thomson), xxiii
Hope (merchant ship), 63
Howe, Robert, 12
Howe, Sir William, xxxii
Howell, David, 39, 40, 41, 65, 66,
  67, 69, 70-71, 78, 80, 87, 88-91
Humphreys, Daniel, 18
Huntington, Benjamin, 34
Huntington, Samuel, 34

Impost, xxxviii, xxxix, 70-71
Independence Day, 14-16

*Independent Gazeteer; or, The Chroni-
  cle of Freedom*, 18
Indian affairs, 68, 70, 82-83, 85,
  86
Izard, Ralph, 8, 24, 25, 74, 79, 80,
  81

Jackson, William, 20
Jay, John, xxi, xxxvi, 70
Jefferson, Thomas, xxxi, xxxii,
  xxxvi, 67
Jenings, Edmund, 92
Jones, John Paul, 55
Jones, Joseph, 46, 49
Jordan, John, 55

La Luzerne, Anne-César, Cheva-
  lier de, xlv, 3, 10, 17, 40, 90, 94
Laurens, Henry, 92
Lawrence (Laurens), Thomas, 17,
  76-77, 92
Lee, Arthur, xx, 53, 64, 67
Lee, Richard Henry, xxxi, xxxiii
Letters from a Pennsylvania Farmer
  (John Dickinson), 6
Libertas Americana medal, 56
Lincoln, Benjamin, 12
Livingston, Susannah French
  (Mrs. William Livingston), 22
Livingston, William, 22
Lloyd, N., 48
Lloyd, Peter Zachary, 13, 18

McClenachan, Amelia Sophie Har-
  rison (Mrs. Robert Mc-
  Clenachan), 13, 18, 22
McClenachan, Robert, 13, 22, 36,
  47, 49, 77
McDougall, Alexander, 56
McHenry, James, 41, 60, 75
McKinsey, James, 55
Madison, James, 40, 46, 49, 60,
  68, 85
Marine Department, 55, 56-57, 60
Martinique, 63
Maryland, xxvii, xxxiii, xxxvii, 30,